Cooking with Wisdom

A Collection of Naturally Delicious Recipes

BILL AND SYLVIA FERRIN

COOKING WITH WISDOM
A Collection of Naturally Delicious Recipes

Copyright © 2010 by Bill and Sylvia Ferrin

Printed in the United States of America.

ISBN 978-0-9800943-1-2

Cover design by Chase Stamp (www.chasestamp.com)

Author photograph by Paulina Carmel De Castro

Peace Publications (Isaiah 52:7) – A Branch of
Compassion Ministries, St. Charles, MO

To order additional copies:
Call – (314) 440-3975
E-mail – sylviaferrin@hotmail.com
Write – 1316 Pine Bluff Drive, St. Charles, MO 63304

CONTENTS

WELCOME

Welcome to the wonderful world of wholesome cooking, where nutritious food does not taste like sawdust! We invite you to enter our kitchen and share the fun as we prepare delicious, nourishing meals.

Many people want to eat healthier and take better care of their bodies but they don't know where to start. Designed to accompany *Food for Thought – A Healthy Temple for a Holy God*, this cookbook will help you gently transition to a healthier lifestyle. We hope you find it practical and unintimidating.

Some of the recipes in *Cooking with Wisdom* are healthy variations of old favorites. Others will invite you to indulge in new culinary adventures. *Cooking with Wisdom* blends familiar with unfamiliar, old with new, traditional with creative. All of them encourage the use of fresh, natural and organic ingredients.
You'll discover that cooking nourishing meals can be fun and rewarding. As you replace unhealthy foods with more nutritious options, your conscientious choices will yield gratifying benefits. You will also realize that good-for-you foods can taste good too!

We did not design *Cooking with Wisdom* as the epitome of wholesome cooking; it is a transitional tool. Our desire is that these recipes will compel you to eventually go beyond them and learn even more about the wonderful world of whole foods and healthy eating. We hope our recipes encourage you to learn to prepare foods free of chemical additives, unnatural preservatives, and artificial ingredients. For better health, we must minimize our dependence on manmade food substitutes.

Some recipes in this cookbook may not be quite as sweet as you are currently used to. As you give your taste buds a chance to transition, at some point you may find the need to cut back even more on the amount of sweetener called for in some of the recipes.

Keep in mind that we are all unique individuals. God did not create us with a cookie cutter. Our physical needs are not the same. Neither are our taste buds all the same.

We spent many happy hours experimenting with our recipes until we achieved what we perceive to be balanced combinations of flavor and nutrition.

But we believe in creativity in the kitchen! If you follow a *Cooking with Wisdom* recipe but find it does not suit you the way we created it, tweak it in the next time you use it. (Just try to keep it healthy!)

Though most of these recipes are our own creations, some were contributed by others. We included their names with the recipes they so graciously provided.

Cooking delicious, nourishing meals can be fun and rewarding. Join us on our progressive journey, as we strive to become healthier habitats for our holy God.

Happy Cooking!

Bill and Sylvia Ferrin

APPETIZERS AND SNACKS

BEAN-CHEESE DIP

1/4 cup fresh salsa
  2 cups organic refried beans
  4 oz sharp or extra sharp cheddar cheese, grated
1/4 cup cilantro, chopped
   Whole grain tortilla chips

Combine salsa, beans, and cheese in small saucepan. Heat a few minutes, until cheese melts and mixture is warm. Top with cilantro. Serve immediately with chips.

~ This is a big hit with guests and it's easy too!

Enjoy the Journey

Though we know some very health conscious people, we have yet to meet a person who eats perfectly all the time. We live in an imperfect world. Having the mindset that we must have an absolutely perfect diet 100% of the time is unrealistic and will produce disappointment and a sense of failure.

If we do the right things most of the time, occasional deviations from our regular eating habits will do minimal damage.

Rather than setting a goal of absolute perfection, we should rely on God's help and grace as we strive to become better stewards of these bodies He has given us to live in.

BILL'S SPICY ROASTED PECANS

    4 cups pecans
1/4 tsp cayenne pepper
1/2 tsp cinnamon
1/2 tsp paprika
1/2 tsp garlic powder
3/4 tsp ground cumin
    1 tsp salt
    1 Tbsp olive oil
    2 Tbsp unsalted butter
    2 Tbsp organic Worcestershire sauce
1/4 cup grated Parmesan cheese

Preheat oven to 325°.

In small bowl, mix together cayenne pepper, cinnamon, paprika, garlic powder, cumin, and salt; set aside.

In medium saucepan, heat olive oil and butter; stir in Worcestershire sauce. Stir in pecans till well coated with olive oil mixture. Sprinkle blended spices over pecans, a little at a time, stirring to ensure even distribution.

Evenly spread pecans onto baking sheet. Bake 15 minutes, stirring twice while roasting. Transfer pecans to medium non-plastic bowl; immediately toss with cheese.

~ If you like spicy foods and you like pecans, you will definitely like these.

Stay Organized

To enhance productivity and to maintain a calm work environment, keep your pantry, cabinets, and refrigerator organized and clean.

BLACKEYED PEA SALSA

1 15-oz can organic blackeyed peas
1 small jalapeno pepper, seeded and minced
1/4 cup minced fresh cilantro leaves
1/2 cup minced red onion
1-1/2 cups cored, seeded, and finely chopped tomatoes
1 celery stalk, finely diced
2 tsp extra virgin olive oil
1-1/2 Tbsp raw apple cider vinegar
1/4 tsp ground cumin
Salt, to taste
Whole grain tortilla chips

Place blackeyed peas in sieve and rinse them well under cold water; drain excess water and place peas in a bowl. Stir in jalapeno, cilantro, onion, tomatoes, celery, olive oil, vinegar, cumin, and salt.

Serve with whole grain tortilla chips.

~ We know blackeyed peas are not normally used in salsa. But you will probably like this salsa, even if you are not a big fan of blackeyed peas. We think blackeyed peas are tasty and the black "eyes" make the beans interesting to look at too. Give them center stage in this salsa, with the other ingredients backing them up...the result is a delightful snack!

Poetic Moment

When you need a little snack,
Make sure you stay on track.

Choose a snack that's good for you,
Not one that will make you blue.

BRUSCHETTA

2 medium tomatoes, diced
2 cloves garlic, minced
1/4 cup finely chopped onion
1 tsp dried basil
  or 1 bunch (about 3/4 cup chopped) fresh basil
1/2 tsp sea salt
1/4 tsp pepper
1/2 loaf whole grain French or Italian bread, sliced
  Extra virgin olive oil
  Garlic salt

In a small bowl, mix together tomatoes, garlic, onion, basil, salt, and pepper.

Brush bread with olive oil and sprinkle with garlic salt; toast bread in oven or toaster oven. Immediately top with tomato mixture and serve.

~ This is especially good when tomatoes are fresh and in season. Bruschetta is perfect when days are hot and taste buds wane. It's fresh, light and easy to prepare.

Take Time to be Thankful

"God is great, God is good;
Let us thank Him for our food.
By His hands we all are fed;
Give us, Lord, our daily bread."

Traditional Children's Prayer

Take time to thank God for your food.
It acknowledges dependence on Him.
He is the One who provides us with food to eat.

FRESH SALSA*

3 fresh garlic cloves, peeled and pressed
1 large yellow onion, chopped
1 large purple onion, chopped
3 green bell peppers, seeded and coarsely chopped
1 each yellow, orange, and red bell peppers,
    seeded and coarsely chopped
8 to 10 Roma tomatoes, chopped small
2 to 3 garden variety tomatoes, chopped small
5 to 6 jalapeno peppers, finely chopped (Leave seeds.)
1/2 cup corn
    (Shucked fresh off the cob and cooked is best.)
20 cilantro sprigs, chopped fine
    or 1 heaping Tbsp dried cilantro
1 cup black beans, soaked, cooked, and drained
2 scant Tbsp sea salt
2 Tbsp fresh lemon juice
1/3 cup vinegar
    Tabasco or hot sauce, to taste
    (start with 1-1/2 tsp)

Use non-metallic utensils to combine all ingredients in a non-metallic bowl. Refrigerate. Prepare a day before serving.

Enjoy with colorful blue corn tortilla chips.

Makes 4 quarts

~ This salsa requires a lot of chopping but the result is well worth the preparation time. It is the best, freshest salsa we have ever tasted.

* Original Recipe Contributed by Melanie Chandler. We altered it slightly.

GUACAMOLE

2 avocadoes, peeled, pitted, and mashed (or chopped)
2 cloves garlic, crushed
1/8 tsp cayenne pepper or 1/2 tsp jalapeno peppers, seeded and finely chopped
1/2 tsp sea salt
1 Tbsp fresh lemon or lime juice
1 Tbsp finely chopped cilantro
2 Tbsp finely chopped red onions or scallions
1/2 cup peeled, seeded, and diced tomatoes

Mix together all ingredients. Refrigerate at least one hour before serving with whole grain tortilla chips.

~ Optional additions: Black pepper, dash of paprika, dash of hot sauce, pinch of cumin, chopped and roasted red bell peppers.

~ Guacamole is best eaten fresh. If not eaten fresh, the lemon will preserve it for a while, but it will lose some of its flavor.

Spiritual Health

A healthy body is only one component of a healthy human life. Fran Lebowitz said "Food is an important part of a balanced diet." In our pursuit of better physical health, we must be careful to not neglect our spiritual health. How we care for our spiritual man has eternal implications.

Cicero stated it well: "Diseases of the soul are more dangerous and more numerous than those of the body."

HUMMUS

1 15-oz can (1-1/2 cups) garbanzo beans
        (chickpeas), shelled (Reserve water.)
1/2 tsp cumin
1/2 tsp paprika
1/2 tsp sea salt
    3 cloves garlic, minced
1/2 Tbsp balsamic vinegar
    1 Tbsp olive oil
1-1/2 Tbsp tahini
2-1/2 Tbsp lemon juice
    2 Tbsp reserved water from chickpeas

Place garbanzo beans in a bowl and mash with a fork or potato masher. Transfer beans and all other ingredients to mixer or blender; process till smooth. (If you have a food processor, use it to make hummus. Your hummus will be smoother if made in a food processor.)

Makes 1-1/2 cups

~ Hummus is great served on toasted French bread or used as a dip with pita chips. You can also put the hummus inside a pita wrap for a unique sandwich. I like to lightly toast sprouted grain tortillas, break them apart, and serve them with the hummus.

~ Garbanzo beans, the chief ingredient in hummus, are a good source of iron, low in sodium, and high in fiber.

Lemon Juice

To extract more juice from a lemon, warm it in the
oven for few minutes before squeezing,
or allow it to warm to room temperature.
Also, lemons that are less firm will have more juice.

MAPLE PECANS

1 cup raw pecans
2 Tbsp butter
1/3 cup pure maple syrup

In a small saucepan, melt butter. Add maple syrup and mix well. Add pecans and stir until coated.

Place pecans on a large cookie sheet. Bake at 350° for 30 to 45 minutes or until maple syrup crystallizes. Stir pecans once every 10 minutes and every 5 minutes right before maple syrup begins to crystallize.

~ Remove pecans from oven before syrup turns dark brown; the dark color is an indication that pecans are beginning to burn.

Surprise! Great Tasting Food!

Many people are pleasantly surprised that they really like the food we prepare. Perhaps they expect unidentifiable dry and tasteless food.

What is our secret to cooking food that even non-health nuts enjoy? First, we cook meals from scratch most of the time so the food is fresh. Also, we use many spices and homemade sauces. We pair unusual foods together to discover delightful blends of flavors. Our idea is this: If we have to cook and we have to eat, why not make the food as nutritious and delicious as possible? God gave us taste buds. Why should we punish them by eating bland food? Besides all that, cooking delicious food is fun!

MEXICAN LAYER DIP

1 15-oz can organic refried beans
1 packet organic taco seasoning
1/4 cup sliced green onions
1 cup sour cream
1 cup picante sauce or salsa
3/4 cup spicy guacamole
1 cup shredded sharp or extra sharp cheddar cheese
1/2 cup black olives
2 medium tomatoes, chopped

Evenly spread refried beans into a shallow dish. Sprinkle desired amount of taco seasoning over the beans. Layer all other ingredients, except the tomatoes, in the order given. Chill. Arrange tomatoes on top just before serving.

Serve with tortilla chips.

~ Shredded lettuce and sliced jalapeno peppers may be added as well.

~ I have a hunch that native Mexicans may have never heard of this dip, but I could be wrong. Either way, it is a quick, easy appetizer or snack.

Preventative Maintenance

Think eating healthy is expensive? It's actually cheap...when you compare it to the cost of doctors, hospitals, and surgeries.

"An ounce of prevention is worth a pound of cure." That statement is as true today as when Benjamin Franklin coined it about 300 years ago.

SMOKED SALMON SPREAD

4 Tbsp butter, softened
8 oz cream cheese, softened
8 oz smoked salmon, coarsely chopped
 (We use All Natural Echo Farms Wild Alaskan
 Sockeye Salmon – Cajun Flavor.)
1/4 tsp seasoning salt
 (We use Simply Organic Hot and Spicy Salt.)
1/2 tsp organic Worcestershire sauce
1/2 tsp hot pepper sauce
 1 tsp minced garlic
 4 Tbsp green onions, minced
1/4 cup fresh dill or 1 Tbsp dried dill

Combine all ingredients, except salmon, and mix together. Add salmon last. Cover and refrigerate for at least two hours before serving. Serve with crackers.

~ Store in the refrigerator for up to three days.

~ Before serving, allow spread to soften at room temperature for about 20 minutes.

Eat Out

There is something enjoyable about eating outdoors during pleasant weather.

If you work indoors, take your lunch break outside. Go picnicking occasionally. If you have a porch or deck, use it often to serve meals. Eating breakfast outside, while the day is still and quiet, is mentally relaxing and a good time to read and think about the goodness of God.

TZATZIKI

1/2 Tbsp extra virgin olive oil
2 tsp wine vinegar
2 cloves garlic, finely chopped
1/2 tsp sea salt
1/2 tsp white pepper
1/2 cup plain yogurt
1/2 cup organic sour cream
1 cucumber, peeled, seeded, and finely diced
1 tsp fresh dill

Combine olive oil, vinegar, garlic, salt, and pepper; mix well. In a separate bowl, blend together yogurt and sour cream. Add the oil mixture and stir. Add cucumbers and mix all ingredients well. Chill. Sprinkle with dill just before serving. Serve with lightly toasted pita bread.

Once served, black pepper is a great complement to tzatziki.

~ Tzatziki is a delicious, traditional Greek dish.

Heartwarming Health

A superb meal does not require the finest china or new dining room furniture. The food does not have to be fancy or expensive, just fresh and healthy and prepared with love and generosity.
A meal where smiles abound and people are genuinely interested in one another is the best kind of meal. This kind of meal not only feeds the body but warms the heart.

QUICK SNACK IDEAS

All-natural smoked trout or smoked salmon
on whole grain crackers

Olives

Celery sticks with raw organic almond butter

A handful of raw almonds, cashews, sunflower seeds, or
pumpkin seeds

Pomegranate seeds

Avocado slices

Cottage cheese with peaches or other fruit

Guacamole with baked tortillas, broken into pieces

Hard boiled or deviled eggs

Fresh cut, mixed fruit such as watermelon, cantaloupe,
honeydew melon, strawberries, blueberries, raspberries,
bananas, kiwi, oranges, pineapple, peaches, and
nectarines

Halved, pitted Medjool dates stuffed with raw walnuts

Unsulfured, unsweetened dried fruit such as figs,
raisins, and mango

Hummus on whole grain pita bread

Slices of raw cheese with whole grain crackers

Plain yogurt with fresh berries and maple syrup

Homemade trail mix with nuts and unsulphured,
unsweetened dried fruit of your choice

Artisan bread dipped in olive oil with balsamic vinegar,
grated parmesan cheese and black pepper

$ Money Saving Tip $

Do it yourself.

Order a slice or two of apple pie at a restaurant. Or, make an apple pie at home. For about the same price, you can choose between a couple of slices and an entire pie. Buy soup for your family at a restaurant or a grocery store's prepared food department. Or make your own and you will have an entire pot of soup for less. Examples like these could go on and on.

It is rare to come up short when you do-it-yourself. It is almost always cheaper than eating out or buying prepared foods. According to statistics published on www.forbes.com, the average American spends 13.3% of his or her annual budget on food. Astoundingly, 42% of that is spent in restaurants! It's a misconception that healthy food is expensive.

What do you need to eat affordably and healthily? Good meal planning and thrifty shopping. And of course, you must be willing to regularly invest your time and energy in the kitchen to prepare homemade meals.

SALADS
AND
SALAD DRESSINGS

AVOCADO RANCH DRESSING

1 avocado, peeled and pitted
1/2 cup milk
1 cup buttermilk
2 Tbsp chopped fresh herbs, such as tarragon
       and/or chives
1 tsp apple cider vinegar
1 tsp balsamic vinegar
2 tsp minced anchovy fillet or 1/2 tsp salt

Puree all ingredients in blender until smooth.

Makes 1-1/2 cups

~ Make this dressing as needed. It does not retain its delicious flavor if used later.

How to Cut an Avocado

Use a sharp knife to cut lengthwise around the avocado, through the skin and meat all the way to the pit. You will now have two avocado halves.

Fold a kitchen towel and use it to hold the avocado half with the pit. Very gently, make a shallow X in the pit with a knife. Keep the knife in one of the lines and use it to gently twist the pit. It should loosen easily. (Be very careful so the knife does not slip and cut your hand.)

Use a spoon to loosen the meat from the skin. Depending on what the avocado will be used for, you can now make lengthwise slices, or cut it into squares, while it is still in the skin. Use a spoon to remove the avocado slices or squares.

CAESAR SALAD

Romaine lettuce
Croutons (See page 26)
Caesar Salad Dressing
Freshly grated Parmesan cheese
Fresh ground black pepper

Place desired amount of lettuce and croutons in large bowl. Toss with Caesar Salad Dressing until salad is thoroughly coated. Place salad on individual plates. Top each salad with Parmesan cheese and pepper.

~ This is a light, but filling salad. Guests love it! Add grilled chicken tenders for a terrific main meal.

Caesar Salad Dressing

3 cloves garlic, minced
1 tsp organic Worcestershire sauce
1 tsp anchovy paste
1 tsp Dijon mustard
2 tsp fresh squeezed lemon juice
1/2 cup freshly grated Parmesan cheese
1 cup mayonnaise (See page 191)

In a bowl, whisk together all ingredients. Cover and refrigerate at least 2 hours before serving.

Makes about 1 cup

Royal Estate

"I had rather be on my farm
than be emperor of the world."

George Washington

CHILLED LENTIL SALAD

3 cups cooked brown lentils, cooled
1/4 cup chopped green bell pepper
1/4 cup chopped red bell pepper
1/4 cup chopped carrots
1/4 cup chopped celery
1/4 cup chopped onions
1/2 cup olive oil
3 Tbsp lemon juice
3 cloves minced garlic
1/2 Tbsp honey
1 cup fresh tomatoes, diced
    or canned fire roasted tomatoes
    Herbamare or other herbal seasoning blend
    Fresh ground black pepper

Combine green bell pepper, red bell pepper, carrots, celery, and onions. Add to lentils.

In small bowl, mix olive oil, lemon juice, garlic, and honey; add to lentils. Then add tomatoes to lentils and season with Herbamare and pepper, to taste.

Chill before serving.

Serves 4

~ This salad is colorful and healthy.

~ Double or triple this salad to serve larger groups...or to have delicious leftovers!

Go for the Garlic

"There is no such thing as a little garlic."

Arthur Baer

CRANBERRY SALAD/RELISH

2 cups coarsely chopped fresh cranberries
2 oranges, peeled, seeded, and coarsely chopped
2 apples, peeled, seeded, and cubed
1/2 cup walnuts, coarsely chopped
1/4 cup honey
1/4 cup maple syrup
1 tsp cinnamon

Mix all ingredients. Place in the refrigerator to allow flavors to blend.

~ This cranberry relish is wonderful. It is delicious enough to stand on its own as a salad or be served on the side as a relish. Try making it for your Thanksgiving dinner; your guests might prefer it to traditional canned cranberry sauce. A friend suggested that it be used on sandwich bread or tortillas with turkey, sliced avocado, and gorgonzola cheese.

Serves 8 to 10

Finest Foods

"It is vitally important that we can continue to say, with absolute conviction, that organic farming delivers the highest quality, best-tasting food, produced without artificial chemicals or genetic modification, and with respect for animal welfare and the environment, while helping to maintain the landscape and rural communities."

Prince Charles

CROUTONS*

Day old whole loaf (not sliced) whole wheat bread
Extra virgin olive oil
Sea salt
Dried parsley
Garlic powder

Preheat oven to 375° using convection setting.

In small bowl, mix together salt, parsley, and garlic powder. Cut bread into cubes and place in large bowl. Drizzle bread cubes with olive oil and toss until evenly coated with oil. Sprinkle spice mixture onto bread cubes and toss to evenly coat with spices.

Spread cubed, seasoned bread onto cookie sheet and bake until slightly crunchy, about 15 minutes, tossing with a spatula a couple times during baking.

Use as a complement to soup or salads.

* Recipe Contributed by Carmel Capotosto

$ Money Saving Tip $

Don't pay someone else to do what you can do.

Rather than buying ready-to-eat bagged lettuce, buy whole lettuce; wash and prepare as needed. Make your own salad dressings. Instead of buying shredded cheese, buy a block of cheese and shred it yourself. Doing such simple things saves money and is not as time consuming or labor intensive as some people think.

ISRAELI SALAD

3/4 cup cored and diced tomatoes
3/4 cup diced cucumber
     (If the skin is tender, leave it on.)
1/2 cup chopped red bell pepper

Dressing:
  1 tsp extra virgin olive oil
  2 tsp lemon juice
    Salt and pepper, to taste

Optional Ingredients:
1/4 cup green, orange, or yellow bell pepper
3/4 cup carrots
  1 Tbsp finely chopped scallions
1/2 Tbsp chopped flat leaf parsley

In a glass bowl, combine tomatoes and cucumbers. (These vegetables create the traditional Israeli salad.) Add red bell pepper and any desired optional ingredients.

Just before serving, stir in olive oil, lemon, salt and pepper. This salad is best eaten fresh.

~ Don't omit the salt and pepper. They nicely bring out the flavor of the vegetables. Also, try to cut the vegetables in even cubes as small as possible. This is part of what makes the salad uniquely Israeli.

~ Israelis love this salad, even for breakfast with a selection of olives, yogurt, cheese, eggs, and bread. It may sound strange but trust me, it is delicious. We have great memories of eating breakfast on the verandah of a guesthouse overlooking the Sea of Galilee. Please try this salad, whether at breakfast, lunch or dinner. It is easy and very healthy.

MACARONI SALAD

1 green bell pepper, chopped small
1 medium onion, chopped small
2 large or 3 small carrots, chopped small
1 lb whole wheat macaroni shells, cooked and cooled
2 cups mayonnaise (See page 191)
   Homemade sweetened condensed milk (See below)

In a large bowl, combine green bell pepper, onion, carrots, and macaroni shells; set aside.

In a medium bowl, mix together mayonnaise and homemade sweetened condensed milk.

Stir mayonnaise mixture into macaroni mixture. Refrigerate overnight. Mix well before serving.

Makes 13 1-cup servings

~ This macaroni salad always gets rave reviews when we take it to potluck dinners.

Homemade Sweetened Condensed Milk

1/3 cup boiling water
1/3 cup honey
3 Tbsp oil or softened butter
1 cup organic non-instant dry milk powder
1/2 tsp vanilla, optional

Use a blender to combine boiling water, honey, and oil or butter. Add milk powder a little at a time and blend until smooth. Add vanilla, if desired. Refrigerate for 30 minutes before using. This recipe is equivalent to one 14-ounce can sweetened condensed milk.

MAPLE CITRUS VINAIGRETTE SALAD

        8 oz combination of greens
            (We suggest using Romaine and spring mix.)
        3 small boneless skinless chicken breast halves,
            seasoned as desired, grilled, and cooled
            Crumbled bleu or grated raw cheddar cheese
            (Bill recommends raw Maytag bleu cheese.)
            Maple Pecans (See page 15)
        3 Granny Smith apples
    2-1/4 cups Maple Citrus Vinaigrette

Cut chicken into strips. Place two ounces of greens on each of four large plates. Add chicken, cheese, and pecans. Core, peel and thinly slice apples; add to salads. Generously drizzle vinaigrette over each salad.

Serves 4

~ For the sake of time, when preparing the salad, we recommend that the Maple Pecans be made early in the day or the day before serving the salad.

~ We admit that preparing this salad is time consuming, but it is worth the effort! You simply must try this one – the blend of flavors is stupendous!

Maple Citrus Vinaigrette

        1/2 cup pure maple syrup
        2 Tbsp raw apple cider vinegar
        1 tsp fresh basil, finely chopped
        2 Tbsp fresh lemon juice
    1-1/2 cups fresh squeezed Minneola orange juice

In a small bowl, blend together all ingredients. Prepare dressing just prior to serving.

~ We prefer Minneola oranges. If you cannot locate these, choose oranges with a sweet-tart flavor.

OIL AND VINEGAR
HERB SALAD DRESSING*

Extra virgin olive oil
Balsamic vinegar
Garlic salt
Dried thyme
Dried marjoram
Dried oregano
Fresh ground black pepper

Using a 2 to 1 ratio (Example: 2 Tbsp olive oil to 1 Tbsp vinegar), whisk together olive oil and vinegar. Mix in spices, adding the amounts that suit your taste buds.

Prepare this fresh and pour onto salad. Toss and enjoy.

* Contributed by Bea Ferrin

Don't Ignore your Health

From my uncomfortable vantage point in the dental chair, I could see a sign that read, "Ignore your teeth and they will go away." Since that was the only thing to concentrate on – other than the drone of the dentist's drill and the occasional jolt of pain – I was one child that got the message: If I want healthy teeth, I must take action. Robert Orben said something similar: "Quit worrying about your health. It'll go away." The point is that, in our over-indulgent society, we cannot expect to be healthy if we float downstream. We must make conscious and responsible choices.

ORIENTAL COLESLAW

Coleslaw Dressing

1 tsp raw honey
2 Tbsp naturally fermented soy sauce
3 Tbsp rice vinegar
1/3 cup olive oil
1/2 tsp sea salt
1/2 tsp freshly ground black pepper
   Asian Vegetable Ramen noodles seasoning packet
2 Tbsp freshly grated ginger
2 Tbsp scallions, finely chopped
1 clove garlic, peeled and mashed

Coleslaw Salad

1 lb green cabbage, shredded
1/2 cup chopped scallions
2 2.1-oz packages Asian Vegetable Ramen
     noodles, cooked, cooled, and crumbled
1/3 cup raw sunflower seeds
1/4 cup raw almond slivers, toasted

Combine dressing ingredients and mix well. Chill in refrigerator for one hour. Meanwhile, combine salad ingredients in a large bowl. Toss dressing with salad; serve immediately to maintain crunchiness.

Note: If you anticipate leftovers, prepare individual portions and store remaining salad and dressing separately in the refrigerator.

~ Fortunately, there are options to the usual additive and chemical filled Ramen noodles. Purchase only natural, organic Ramen noodles.

~ This dressing is good with sprouts.

ORZO GARDEN SALAD

Orzo Dressing

2 Tbsp Dijon mustard
1/2 cup raw honey
1/2 cup extra virgin olive oil
2/3 cup raw apple cider vinegar
1/2 tsp freshly ground black pepper
    Dash of sea salt

Orzo Salad

2 cups whole wheat orzo pasta, uncooked
    (makes about 5 cups cooked orzo)
2 cups chopped combination of red, green, orange
    and/or yellow bell peppers
1 cup finely chopped scallions
1/4 cup chopped fresh parsley
1/2 cup chopped black and/or Kalamata (Greek)
    olives, depending on preference
1-1/2 cup crumbled feta cheese

Cook orzo in rapidly boiling water according to directions; drain, then rinse with cold water. Place orzo in a large bowl. Add peppers, scallions, and parsley. Place olives and feta cheese in small serving bowls to be added at the table.

In a small bowl, combine mustard and honey. Whisk in olive oil and vinegar. Add pepper and salt. Stir the dressing into the salad. Allow flavors to blend in the refrigerator a couple of hours. Stir salad and serve.

Makes about 9 cups salad

~ For variation, try adding chopped carrots.

~ Orzo resembles rice, but it is a type of pasta.

POPPY SEED SALAD DRESSING

1/3 cup balsamic vinegar
  3 Tbsp raw honey
  1 tsp sea salt
  1 tsp dry mustard
  1 Tbsp grated onions
  1 Tbsp poppy seeds
1/2 cup sunflower, safflower, or olive oil

In a bowl, combine all ingredients *except* the oil. Slowly whisk in the oil.

~ This salad dressing is delicious served over soft lettuce such as Boston or Bibb. Toss in cucumbers, tomatoes, and feta cheese for a refreshingly light salad.

Makes 1 cup

$ Money Saving Tip $

Plan your meals.

Plan your meals for a week.
Then make a list of ingredients you need to buy.

Making meal plans will accomplish three things:
1. You will save money by not throwing away food that goes bad before you use it.
2. You will be organized and focused.
3. You will not have to wonder, "What should I cook this week?" while standing in the store.

POTATO SALAD WITH FRESH HERBS

2 lb small red potatoes, halved
2 lb Yukon gold potatoes, cut into 1-inch cubes
3/4 cup plain yogurt
3/4 cup mayonnaise (See page 191)
2 garlic cloves, chopped
1/2 cup chopped sweet onions
1 tsp honey
1 tsp organic Worcestershire sauce
2 Tbsp lemon juice
1/4 tsp black pepper
1/2 tsp dry mustard
1/2 tsp cayenne pepper
1 tsp salt
1/8 cup finely chopped fresh dill
1/4 cup coarsely chopped fresh basil
1/4 cup coarsely chopped fresh chives
1/4 cup coarsely chopped fresh parsley

Gently boil potatoes until tender, approximately 25 minutes. Drain and cool to room temperature.

While potatoes are boiling, combine yogurt, mayonnaise, garlic, sweet onions, honey, Worcestershire sauce, lemon juice, black pepper, dry mustard, cayenne pepper, and salt in a small bowl; refrigerate.

Chop fresh herbs and place in another small bowl.

When potatoes are cool, in a large bowl combine potatoes, sauce, and herbs. Allow to chill for at least two hours before serving.

~ This is quite different from the usual potluck potato salad. The Yukon gold potatoes and fresh herbs give it a "fresh from the field" flavor.

RASPBERRY MAPLE VINAIGRETTE*

1/2 cup raw apple cider vinegar
1/2 cup balsamic vinegar
1/2 cup seedless raspberry fruit spread
1/2 cup pure maple syrup
  1 cup extra virgin olive oil
  2 tsp dried mustard
  2 tsp sea salt

Whisk together vinegars, fruit spread, and maple syrup. Add olive oil, mustard and salt. Stir until blended.

We recommend serving this vinaigrette with the following salad:
Organic baby spinach leaves
Matchstick carrots
Red onion, thinly sliced
Roasted pistachio meats
Dried cranberries
Gorgonzola or blue cheese, if desired
Grilled chicken breast, if desired

~ This dressing is excellent, a good sweet-tart blend. Purchase fruit spread that does not have added sugar or artificial sweetener. Fruit-only fruit spread is best.

* Recipe Contributed by Carmel Capotosto

Poetic Moment

Fresh from our gardens onto the plates,
Lettuce and tomatoes make good mates.

Add some dressing to make it valid,
And you'll have the perfect salad.

SUMMER SALAD

1/2 cup boneless, skinless chicken breasts or tenders
1/4 cup slivered almonds
2/3 cup feta cheese, crumbled
   1 cup sliced organic strawberries, fresh or frozen
   3 cups (packed) mixed greens
3/4 cup raspberry maple vinaigrette (See page 35)

Liberally season chicken with sea salt, fresh ground pepper, and garlic powder. Put 1 tablespoon oil in small pan, add chicken and cook. Allow to cool, then shred or slice into bite sized pieces.

Measure all ingredients into a bowl, toss with salad dressing, and serve.

Makes 2 large entrée salads or 6 side/dinner salads.

~ This is a delightfully delicious salad that you probably will not want to relegate to hot summers only, but enjoy year 'round! It is one of our favorites.

Piles of Smiles

Question:
What did the carrot say to the wheat?

Answer:
"Lettuce rest, I'm feeling beet."

Shel Silverstein

SYLVIA'S SALAD DRESSING

1/8 tsp garlic powder
1/8 tsp Herbamare or other herbal seasoning blend
  1 tsp honey mustard (See page 182)
  1 tsp soy sauce
  2 tsp honey
  2 Tbsp balsamic vinegar
  2 Tbsp apple cider vinegar
1/2 cup extra virgin olive oil

Whisk together all ingredients. Refrigerate until needed.

Makes 1 cup

Beyond Iceberg

Iceberg lettuce is the only type of lettuce many people buy. Unfortunately, it is also the least nutritious...and the least tasty. Other types of lettuce are significantly higher in vitamins, especially vitamins A and K. To boost your vitamin intake and give more flavor to your salads and sandwiches, branch out beyond iceberg lettuce to some greener options.

Romaine is crisp and sturdy. It is great with nearly any kind of dressing, whether light or heavy. Green leaf lettuce and red-tipped leaf lettuce have curly edges, which add interest to salads. They are great on sandwiches also. Boston (or butter) and bibb are nice, sweet, tender types of lettuce. Arugula is a lettuce with a strong flavor. It is best used to accent other lettuce in a salad.

TABOULI

3/4 cup bulgur
  1 clove garlic, crushed
  1 tsp freshly cracked black pepper
1-1/2 tsp sea salt
  1/4 cup fresh lemon juice
  1/4 cup extra virgin olive oil
  1/4 cup fresh mint leaves, finely chopped
  3/4 cup scallions, white and green parts, chopped
  2 cups (packed) freshly chopped parsley
  2 medium tomatoes, peeled, seeded, and diced

Optional Ingredients:
1/2 cup cooked chickpeas
1/2 cup coarsely grated carrots
  1 green bell pepper, chopped
  1 cucumber, peeled, seeded, and chopped

Add bulgur wheat to 1-1/2 cups boiling water. Simmer over low heat for 20 to 25 minutes, until bulgur is chewable. Let stand for 10 minutes, covered; cool.

Add garlic, pepper, salt, lemon juice, olive oil, and mint. Mix thoroughly. Refrigerate 2 to 3 hours.

Just prior to serving, add the scallions, parsley, and tomatoes; mix gently.

Serve with feta cheese and olives, if desired. Tabouli is also great with whole grain tortilla chips.

~ Though a longer cooking time may be necessary, cracked wheat may be used instead of bulgur.

TOMATO-ONION-CUCUMBER SALAD

2 large tomatoes, chopped
1/2 cup cucumber, seeds removed and chopped
1 cup onions, chopped
6 Tbsp extra virgin olive oil
2 Tbsp balsamic vinegar
1 Tbsp raw apple cider vinegar

Combine all ingredients in medium sized bowl. Season to taste with fresh ground pepper, sea salt, garlic powder, and marjoram. Allow flavors to blend in refrigerator for at least 1 hour before serving.

~ This salad is also great on toasted whole grain French bread.

Terrific Tomatoes

There is nothing quite as delicious as fresh tomatoes. Here's how to dress up your tomatoes for a delightful lunch or snack:

Thickly slice fresh organic tomatoes. Pour Bragg Organic Healthy Vinaigrette lightly over tomatoes, then place small amounts of chèvre (soft goat cheese – pronounced "shev") on them. Grind black pepper over tomatoes.

Take our word on this one: "It's delicious!!!"

(Bragg Vinaigrette is a nice combination of apple cider vinegar, olive oil, and spices. If you do not have any on hand, use Oil and Vinegar Herb Salad Dressing instead (See page 30).

WALDORF TURKEY SALAD SANDWICHES

    3 cups cooked turkey, cut into bite-sized pieces
    1 cup red grapes, cut in half, seeds removed
    1 cup seeded, peeled, and diced apple,
        tossed with 1 Tbsp orange juice
3/4 cup chopped walnuts
1/2 cup mayonnaise (See page 191)
1/2 tsp sea salt
1/4 tsp pepper

Combine all ingredients. Cover and chill 2 to 3 hours. Serve on whole-grain bread.

~ Instead of turkey, white and/or dark chicken meat may be used.

~ Vary this recipe by adding one or all of the following: Chopped bell pepper, chopped celery, garlic powder.

$ Money Saving Tip $

Buy food in bulk.

At most health food stores and some grocery stores, you can select spices, beans, grains, nuts, seeds, granola, cereal, honey, and maple syrup from bulk containers.

Buying in bulk usually costs less than buying the same product prepackaged. If you use large quantities of certain staples, such as grains, you can usually order large amounts at significantly discounted prices.

SOUPS

BROCCOLI CHEESE SOUP

2 Tbsp butter
1 Tbsp whole wheat flour
1 tsp sea salt
1 tsp black pepper
5 cups whole milk
2-1/2 cups chopped fresh broccoli
3 tsp chopped green onion
4 tsp Organic Better than Bouillon Chicken Base
2 cups shredded extra-sharp cheddar cheese

Melt butter in saucepan. Stir in flour, salt, and pepper to create a paste; set aside.

Heat milk in large saucepan. Add broccoli, onions, Better than Bouillon Chicken Base, and butter mixture; cook till vegetables are tender and soup is thickened.

If the cheese gets too hot when added, the oils in the cheese will separate. Before adding cheese, remove soup from burner and allow soup to cool a little. If you prefer, you can add the cheese to the soup after it has been placed in serving bowls.

Serves 8

Pay Attention to Details

"The failure or incomplete success of a recipe oftentimes depends upon some little detail that has been misunderstood or overlooked in the preparation."

A Book for a Cook, The Pillsbury Co. (1905)

BUTTERNUT SQUASH SOUP

4 Tbsp unsalted butter
2 large cloves garlic, minced
3 cups chopped onions
2 tsp fresh sage, chopped
1/2 tsp ground cloves
3/4 tsp ground nutmeg
3/4 tsp sea salt
1 tsp ground cinnamon
Freshly ground pepper, to taste
1 Granny Smith apple, peeled, seeded, and diced
4 lb butternut squash, peeled, seeded,
    and cut into 1-inch chunks
5 cups chicken stock, reserve one cup
    (Additional chicken stock may be needed to thin
    the soup when it is almost finished.)
1/2 cup light cream or half and half
1/2 cup pure maple syrup

In a large pot, melt butter over medium-low heat; add the garlic and onions and cook until onions are soft and translucent, stirring occasionally. Stir in the sage, cloves, nutmeg, sea salt, cinnamon, and pepper. Add the apple, squash, and four cups of chicken stock. Bring to a boil, reduce heat and simmer, partially covered, for 20 minutes, or till the squash is tender. Remove from heat.

In a blender, puree the soup in batches until smooth. Return to pot and simmer; stir in the cream and maple syrup. Using remaining chicken stock, thin the soup to desired consistency. Simmer 10 minutes and serve.

Freeze soup that will not be consumed within two days.

Makes 10 1-cup servings

~ This is the perfect soup for a chilly fall day.

CHILI

    1 lb ground beef
    1 Tbsp oil
    2 cloves garlic, minced
    1 cup onion, chopped
1/2 cup green bell pepper, chopped
    1 14-oz can tomato sauce
    1 14-oz can diced tomatoes, undrained
    2 cans beans, drained
        (Pinto, kidney, red, white, or a combination)
1/2 tsp pepper
1/2 tsp dried basil
    1 tsp sea salt
    1 Tbsp cumin
2 to 3 Tbsp chili powder
    2 bay leaves

In large pot, cook ground beef till browned; drain fat, remove ground beef from pot and set aside. On low to medium heat, in same pot, add oil, garlic, and onions. Simmer until translucent. Add all other ingredients and bring to low boil; immediately reduce heat and simmer 15 minutes, stirring occasionally.

Serve with shredded cheddar cheese, chopped onions, and oyster crackers, if desired.

~ For less thick chili, use 2 cans tomato sauce. If you like more meat than beans, use only 1 can beans.

Poetic Moment

Piping hot soup, on a chilly day,
That's what keeps the cold at bay.

Have a cup or maybe two,
And you'll feel cozy, through and through.

GAZPACHO

2 cups beef broth or stock
1 cup tomato sauce
2 medium cucumbers, peeled, seeded, finely chopped
1 red onion, finely chopped
1 bunch scallions, finely chopped
1 medium green bell pepper, finely chopped
2 large tomatoes, finely chopped
3 garlic cloves, minced
1/2 cup water
1 Tbsp red wine vinegar
1 Tbsp lemon juice
1/2 tsp Tabasco
2 Tbsp fresh cilantro, finely chopped
2 Tbsp fresh basil, finely chopped
   Sea salt and black pepper to taste
2 tsp organic Worcestershire sauce
2 Tbsp fresh parsley, finely chopped

Bring beef stock and tomato sauce to a boil; cool.

Thoroughly wash all vegetables. Pour the cooled beef stock and tomato sauce into a large non-metallic bowl; add cucumbers, red onion, scallions, green bell pepper, tomatoes, garlic, water, red wine vinegar, lemon juice, Tabasco, cilantro, and basil. Stir until the ingredients are well combined and season with salt and pepper.

Refrigerate at least 4 hours, then add Worcestershire sauce and parsley. Serve gazpacho in chilled bowls.

Serves 6

~ Not everyone likes cold soup; the very words "cold soup" seem like an oxymoron. But for those – like Bill – who do, gazpacho is good indeed, especially on a hot summer day! Gazpacho is light and flavorful. For ultimate flavor, it is best to prepare gazpacho at the peak of the growing season.

HEARTY WEDDING SOUP*

5 Italian chicken sausages, chopped small
3 Tbsp olive oil
4 cloves fresh garlic, diced
1 large onion, diced
3 cups chicken broth
1 28-oz can tomato puree
1 28-oz can black beans
5-6 oz fresh organic baby spinach, coarsely chopped
1/2 tsp black pepper
1/2 tsp dried oregano
1 tsp dried basil
2 tsp sea salt
8 oz small whole grain pasta of choice
Grated Parmesan cheese

In a soup pot, cook chicken sausages in olive oil. Add garlic and onion and sauté just until translucent. (Do not let the garlic get brown.) Add broth, tomato puree, beans (with liquid), spinach and seasonings. To allow the flavors to blend, simmer soup for an hour or two, stirring occasionally.

Just before serving, cook pasta according to package directions in a separate pot; drain, and add to soup.

Serve with a side of Parmesan cheese to be sprinkled over the soup. (For those who wish to avoid dairy products, nutritional yeast can be used in place of the Parmesan cheese.)

Serves 6 to 8

~ This soup is always better if made a day ahead. However, whether you serve the soup right away or wait a day, do not add the pasta to the soup until just prior to serving. This will prevent the pasta from becoming mushy.

HEARTY WEDDING SOUP (Cont.)

~ For a hearty meal on cold days, serve this soup with a green salad and crusty bread. Or, rather than bread, make your own croutons (See page 26) and toss them into the soup.

~ If you partially freeze the chicken sausage, it will be easier to chop.

* Recipe Contributed by Carmel Capotosto

Nona's Perspective on Health

"Our tastes and our eating choices become firmly fixed habits and courage is required to break the mold. It is not easy to go against the grain and against the crowd, but I've decided living to be eighty and feeling like thirty-six is worth it. Of course, I know the calendar will catch up with me one day, but I refuse to sit around and wait for it."

"Isn't it remarkable, folks take better care of their cars and lawn mowers than they do of their bodies? The same people who would not consider using inadequate fuel for their vehicles, poke constant fun at the few "health nuts" who realize that trying to maintain a healthy body on junk is a sad story."

Nona Freeman
Author of *Keeper of the House*

MAINE FISH CHOWDER

Prep Time: 30 minutes
Cook Time: 40 minutes
Total Time: Approximately 1 hour and 10 minutes

1/4 cup butter
2 medium onions, chopped
3 cups peeled potatoes (cut into 3/8-inch squares)
1/2 cup water
5 cups whole milk
1/2 pt heavy cream
2 tsp Organic Better than Bouillon Chicken Base
1/8 tsp curry powder
2 tsp honey
1 lb haddock (cut into 1-inch squares)
1 lb cod (cut into 1-inch squares)
Pepper, to taste

Prior to cooking, cut onions, potatoes, haddock and cod.

In a large stockpot, melt butter on low heat. Add onions and simmer, covered, until translucent and soft, approximately 15 minutes. Stir occasionally.

Add potatoes, water and enough milk to cover potatoes. Bring heat to low boil then cook for 10 minutes. Continue stirring and scraping the bottom of pot every few minutes so the milk and food will not burn.

Add remainder of milk, heavy cream, Better than Bouillon Chicken Base, curry powder and honey. Bring back to a low boil. Then add haddock and cod. Resume low boil then turn heat down and simmer for additional 15 minutes. Serve immediately. Add pepper.

Makes about 13 6-ounce cups or 8 10-ounce bowls

~ This chowder freezes well. (Thaw chowder, then reheat slowly.)

POTATO LEEK SOUP

3 Tbsp butter
4 cloves garlic, crushed
1 large onion, chopped
4 leeks, white and pale green parts,
    sliced into 1/4-inch slices
1/2 tsp sca salt
1/4 tsp pepper
2 Tbsp flour
4 to 5 tsp Organic Better than Bouillon Chicken Base,
    to taste
4 cups water
2 lb Yukon Gold potatoes, peeled and cubed
1 cup milk

To remove all dirt and grit, carefully rinse sliced leeks in bowl full of cold water.

In a heavy-bottomed soup pot, melt butter on low to medium heat. Add garlic, onion, leeks, salt and pepper; cover and cook until soft and translucent, stirring often. Stir in flour; cook for two minutes, then stir in Better than Bouillon Chicken Base.

Add water; bring to a boil. Add potatoes; then, reduce heat and simmer gently for about 40 minutes or until potatoes are soft, stirring occasionally, scraping the bottom of pot. Stir in milk. Remove from heat and cool. Puree soup in blender. Reheat soup slowly and serve.

Serves 6 to 8

~ Instead of Better than Bouillon Chicken Base and water, you may use four cups organic chicken stock or broth. It will not be as flavorful; you may want to add a little Better than Bouillon Chicken Base or more salt.

~ Leftovers freeze well.

SIX BEAN SOUP

1/2 cup dry black beans
1/2 cup dry great northern beans
1/2 cup dry pinto beans
1/2 cup dry soldier beans
1/2 cup dry black eyed peas
15 cups chicken broth
1 tsp cumin
1 Tbsp olive oil
3 bay leaves
4 garlic cloves, chopped
4 cups chopped onions
1 cup brown basmati rice, uncooked
1 cup dry lentils
1/4 tsp freshly ground black pepper
1/2 tsp cayenne pepper
1/2 tsp nutmeg
1 tsp garlic powder
1-1/2 tsp hot sauce
1 to 2 Tbsp natural sweetener of choice

Rinse the first five types of dry beans.

In large pot, bring 10 cups water to a boil; add beans and return to boil for 3 minutes. Turn off heat, cover, and set beans aside for 2 to 4 hours. Drain and discard water; rinse beans.

In the same large pot, boil beans in 15 cups chicken broth for 15 minutes. Add cumin, olive oil, bay leaves, garlic cloves, and onions. Reduce heat to a simmer and cook for 1 hour. Add rice. Cook 1 more hour, or until beans are tender, stirring occasionally. Collect and discard the foam that collects at the top of the pot.

Just before beans are done, add lentils and remaining ingredients. Cook on low heat for 15 to 30 minutes more to allow the flavors to blend and the mixture to thicken.

SIX BEAN SOUP (Cont.)

Depending on how thick you like your soup, you may want to add more chicken broth.

Makes 16 to 20 1-cup servings

~ Soaking beans greatly improves their digestibility. Lentils are an exception, however; they are one of several types of beans that are easily digested and take only a short time to cook.

~ If desired, other types of beans may be used in place of those listed in this recipe. Also, seasoning amounts may be altered to suit individual tastes.

~ This soup can be frozen for later use.

A Meal Fit for King

When David fled Jerusalem, devoted men brought him and his companions provisions to sustain them in the wilderness.

"And it came to pass, when David was come to Mahanaim, that Shobi...and Machir...and Barzillai, Brought beds, and basons, and earthen vessels, and wheat, and barley, and flour, and parched corn, and beans, and lentiles, and parched pulse, And honey, and butter, and sheep, and cheese of kine, for David, and for the people that were with him, to eat: for they said, The people is hungry, and weary, and thirsty, in the wilderness.

II Samuel 17:27-29

SPICY LENTIL SOUP

1 lb dried lentils
1 qt water
2 tsp salt
1 medium onion, chopped
1/4 cup extra virgin olive oil
1 10-oz can diced tomatoes and chilies

In colander, rinse and drain lentils. Place lentils, water, and salt in medium sized pot and cover. Simmer until lentils are tender, about 45 minutes. Check pot frequently and add water if needed.

In small skillet, add oil and onions; simmer until translucent. Add onion, olive oil, and drained tomatoes to the lentils, stirring carefully. Cook lentils for 10 to 15 more minutes. Add more salt if desired.

~ This soup is easy to prepare. It is not a heavy soup, yet it is filling.

Piles of Smiles

Question:
What is the difference between
a hungry man and a glutton?

Answer:
One longs to eat and the other eats too long.

TURKEY TORTILLA SOUP*

1 Tbsp extra virgin olive oil
1 large onion, chopped
1 garlic clove, minced
1 4-oz can diced green chilies
1/2 tsp dried oregano
1 tsp chili powder
1 tsp ground cumin
   Sea salt, to taste
   Black pepper or cayenne pepper, to taste
6 cups turkey or chicken broth
1 28-oz can ground tomatoes
3 cups cooked turkey breast, chopped small
1 cup frozen corn
   Crushed whole grain tortilla chips
   Shredded Monterey Jack cheese, optional
   Chopped pickled jalapenos, optional
   Sour cream, optional

In large soup pot, sauté onion in olive oil until translucent. Add garlic, chilies, oregano, chili powder, cumin, salt and pepper. Stir for one minute. Add broth and tomatoes; bring to a boil.

Reduce to simmer and add turkey and corn. Simmer until corn is cooked, or longer if you want the flavors to blend more.

Ladle hot soup into bowls. Sprinkle tortilla chips over soup and serve with cheese, jalapenos, and sour cream, if desired.

~ Turkey Tortilla Soup can be a way to use leftover turkey.

* Recipe Contributed by Carmel Capotosto

WHITE CHILI

1 Tbsp olive oil
4 garlic cloves, minced
2 medium onions, chopped
2 4-oz cans chopped mild or hot green chilies,
     depending on preference
1/4 tsp ground cloves
1/4 tsp cayenne pepper
1 tsp ground oregano
2 tsp ground cumin
4 cups chicken stock or broth
2 lb boneless, skinless natural chicken breasts or
     tenders, cooked and cut into 1/2-inch pieces
3 15-oz canned Great Northern Beans, drained
     (Canned beans may be used but dry beans that
     have been soaked, then cooked, are preferred.)
20 oz raw Monterey Jack cheese, grated
Organic sour cream
Pickled jalapeno peppers, chopped

In a soup pot, heat oil over low to medium heat. Add garlic and simmer a few minutes. Stir in onions, coating with oil and cook, covered, till translucent; stir occasionally. Stir in chilies, cloves, cayenne pepper, oregano, and cumin; turn up heat and sauté for 2 to 3 minutes. Add stock, chicken, and beans; simmer for 15 minutes.

Add 12 ounces of cheese and continue simmering until cheese is melted.

Ladle chili into large bowls and top with additional cheese as desired. Serve with sides of sour cream and jalapeno peppers.

Serves 6 to 8

~ Depending on your preferences, you may wish to use more chicken broth.

BREAKFAST

BLUEBERRY BREAKFAST CAKE*

2 cups whole spelt flour
1 cup white spelt flour
1-1/3 cups evaporated cane juice granules
2 packets stevia
4 tsp baking powder
2 cups milk
1/2 cup olive oil
2 eggs
2 tsp vanilla
1 lb frozen blueberries

Preheat oven to 350°. Grease a large glass baking dish.

In a large mixing bowl, mix dry ingredients. Make a well in the center.

In a separate bowl, combine wet ingredients, except blueberries. Add wet ingredients to the dry ingredients; mix just till combined. Fold in blueberries with spatula.

Pour batter into baking dish. Sprinkle generously with extra evaporated cane juice to form a sweet crusty top. Bake until done, about 45 minutes to an hour.

* Recipe Contributed by Carmel Capotosto

Enjoy Life

In your food selections, be wise but not obsessive. Some health-conscious people are so consumed with preserving their lives that they don't take time to enjoy them. Maintain your balance.

BLUEBERRY PANCAKES

1 cup whole wheat flour
2 tsp baking powder
1/4 tsp salt
1/2 tsp cinnamon
1 beaten egg
1 cup milk
2 Tbsp oil
1 Tbsp lemon juice, optional
1 cup blueberries

In a small bowl, combine flour, baking powder, salt, and cinnamon. In a large bowl, combine egg, milk, oil, and lemon juice. Gradually stir flour mixture into egg mixture. Gently fold in blueberries.

Pour just enough oil into large pan to coat. Bring to medium heat. Pour in small amounts of batter, leaving a little space between each pancake. When pancakes begin to form little air pockets, flip pancakes and cook until done through.

Makes about 10 4 to 5-inch pancakes

~ To make plain pancakes, simply omit blueberries.

~ If you like fluffier pancakes, add a little more flour. For thinner pancakes, add a little more milk.

~ Try to not over-mix pancake batter. Mix it just until blended.

BREAKFAST BURRITOS

    8 whole grain tortillas
    8 sage flavored chicken sausage links, cooked
        (We use Applegate Farms Breakfast Sausage.)
1/4 cup chopped green onion, sautéed
1/4 cup chopped red bell pepper, sautéed
   12 eggs, scrambled
    1 cup shredded sharp or extra sharp cheddar cheese
      Sour cream
      Salsa

Place all ingredients on table in separate bowls. Allow each person to create their own burritos.

Makes 8 burritos

$ Money Saving Tip $

Buy food that is locally produced.

The average food travels 1500 miles from field to table. Buy fresh, local, seasonal food as much as possible. The fresher the food, the more nutritious and less expensive it will be.
Get fresh food at farmers markets, family operated farm stands, and pick-your-own farms.

Live in a city? Take a drive every couple of weeks into the country to get a supply of fresh, homegrown food that tastes the way food is supposed to taste. You'll get some fresh air too!

EASY EGG CASSEROLE

8 large eggs
4 cups grated raw cheddar cheese
2 4-oz cans diced green chilies
1/4 cup chopped onions, lightly sautéed
1/2 cup any combination of red, green, or orange
bell peppers, chopped and lightly sautéed

Preheat oven to 350°.

Crack eggs into medium bowl and beat. Add cheese, green chilies, onions and peppers; mix together.

Pour mixture into a 9 x 13-inch baking dish and spread evenly across the pan. Bake for about 30 minutes, until the casserole has set and has lightly browned. A toothpick should come out clean.

~ This dish is great for breakfast, brunch, or lunch. If desired, cooked sage flavored chicken sausage may be added.

Seven Species of Divine Provision

"For the LORD thy God bringeth thee into a good land, a land of brooks of water, of fountains and depths that spring out of valleys and hills; A land of wheat, and barley, and vines, and fig trees, and pomegranates; a land of oil olive, and honey;"

Deuteronomy 8:7-8

EXTRA HEALTHY PANCAKES

1 cup freshly ground whole wheat flour
1 cup pure water or homemade yogurt
1 Tbsp whey or lemon juice
1 egg
1/4 tsp sea salt
1/2 tsp cinnamon
1/2 tsp baking soda
1 Tbsp oil or melted butter

In a medium-sized bowl, combine flour, water or yogurt, and whey or lemon juice. Set in a warm place for 12 to 24 hours.

When ready to cook the pancakes, stir all other ingredients into the flour mixture. Cook pancakes on a hot, lightly oiled skillet.

Serve with butter and pure maple syrup.

Makes 15 4-inch pancakes

Buckwheat Pancakes

Instead of 1 cup whole wheat flour, use 1/2 cup whole wheat flour and 1/2 cup buckwheat flour.

Spelt or Kamut Pancakes

Use spelt or kamut flour instead of whole wheat flour.

Strawberry Crepes

Follow all directions but, before cooking, thin the batter with water. Roll sweetened, chopped strawberries and cream cheese in crepes.

GRANOLA*

1 tsp cinnamon
2 tsp baking powder
1 Tbsp ground flax seeds, optional
1 cup whole grain flour of choice
1 to 1-1/2 cups shredded, unsweetened coconut
4 cups rolled oats
1/2 to 1 cup evaporated cane sugar, maple syrup,
or other sweetener
1 to 2 tsp vanilla
1/3 cup oil
1 cup water

Mix dry and wet ingredients separately. Combine and put in a large ungreased baking dish with sides. Bake at 275° to 325°. Stir frequently and cook for 1 to 2 hours.

Allow the granola to cool and serve with plain yogurt and maple syrup. Strawberries or other fruit may be added as well. Delicious!

* Recipe Contributed by Carmel Capotosto, Adapted

Eat Eggs for Energy

Eggs are a great source of energy and are the perfect protein. Plus, they are easy to prepare.

Brighten up your scrambled eggs and omelets by chopping and adding your choice of the following: garlic, onions, scallions, bell peppers, spinach, hard cheeses, cooked chicken, and cooked steak.

SWISS MÜESLI

2 cups rolled oats
1 cup milk
1 Tbsp honey
1 cup plain yogurt
3 Tbsp maple syrup
1 apple, peeled and grated or sliced into narrow strips
1/2 banana, sliced
1 cup blueberries
1 cup strawberries, sliced

Combine oats, milk and honey; cover and soak overnight in the refrigerator.

In the morning, add rest of ingredients in the order given. Stir together and serve.

Serves 4 to 6

~ The following may be added if desired: Sunflower seeds, pumpkin seeds, raisins, dried and unsulfured apricots.

~ We first tasted Swiss Müesli at a bed-and-breakfast in St. Andrews, New Brunswick, Canada. It was so delicious we decided to make it at home.

~ Müesli is best eaten the day it is prepared. It gets slightly soggy and is not as enjoyable when eaten as "leftovers."

The Inexpensive Gift

"If we knew how inexpensive the seeds of kindness are we would scatter them more often."

Unknown

THREE CHEESE
SPINACH AND BROCCOLI QUICHE

3 cups (packed) fresh spinach leaves
3 cups fresh broccoli, chopped
1 unbaked 10-inch pie crust (See page 158)
3/4 cup sharp or extra-sharp cheddar cheese, grated
3/4 cup Swiss cheese, grated
1 cup feta cheese, crumbled
1 Tbsp whole wheat flour
4 eggs, beaten
1-1/2 cups light cream
1/4 cup fresh basil, snipped
Paprika

Preheat oven to 400°. Steam spinach; press excess water out, and chop. Lightly steam broccoli. Set spinach and broccoli aside.

Mix together cheeses in a large bowl. Stir flour into cheeses. Add eggs, cream, basil, spinach, and broccoli; mix well.

Pour the mixture into the pie crust and sprinkle liberally with paprika.

Bake 15 minutes. Lower heat to 325° and bake 25 to 30 minutes longer, until golden. Allow to set at least 15 minutes before slicing and serving.

Serves 4 to 6

White or Brown?

There is no nutritional difference between white or brown eggs. The color of the egg is determined by the color and breed of the bird.

The Garden of Your Daily Life

Plant four rows of peas:
1. Peace of mind
2. Peace of heart
3. Peace of soul
4. Peace with others

Plant four rows of squash:
1. Squash gossip
2. Squash indifference
3. Squash grumbling
4. Squash selfishness

Plant four rows of lettuce:
1. Lettuce be faithful
2. Lettuce be kind
3. Lettuce be patient
4. Lettuce love one another

No good garden is without turnips:
1. Turnip for prayer
2. Turnip for worship
3. Turnip for fellowship
4. Turnip to help others

And every garden needs thyme:
1. Thyme for God
2. Thyme for family
3. Thyme for friends
4. Thyme for strangers

Water your garden with patience and cultivate with love. There will be much fruit from your garden...because we reap what we sow.

Author Unknown (Adapted)

BREADS

BANANA NUT BREAD

1-3/4 cups spelt flour
  1/4 tsp salt
  1/2 tsp baking soda
    2 tsp baking powder (See page 143)
    2 Tbsp milk
  1/3 cup butter or organic, trans fat free all
        vegetable shortening
  1/3 cup honey
    1 cup mashed ripe organic bananas
        (2 to 3 medium bananas)
    2 eggs
  1/2 cup chopped walnuts

In large bowl combine 1 cup of the flour, salt, baking soda, and baking powder. Add milk, butter or shortening, honey, and bananas. Beat with electric mixer on low speed until blended, then on high speed for 2 minutes. Add eggs and remaining flour; beat until blended. Stir in walnuts.

Pour batter into an oiled 8 x 4 x 2-inch loaf pan. Bake in a 350° oven for 55 to 60 minutes or until a toothpick inserted in the center comes out clean. Cool in pan 10 minutes. Remove from pan, cool completely on wire rack; wrap, and store overnight before slicing. (It tastes better eaten the next day.)

Makes 1 loaf

Poetic Moment

The aroma that greets you from fresh baked bread,
Will linger long after the people are fed.

This fresh baked bread will make people say,
"Teach us to make bread the old fashioned way."

BLUEBERRY MUFFINS

      1 cup blueberries
1-3/4 cup plus 2 tsp whole wheat flour
      1 Tbsp baking powder (See page 143)
    1/4 tsp nutmeg
    1/4 tsp cinnamon
      2 eggs, beaten
    1/4 cup oil
    3/4 cup orange juice
      1 tsp lemon or orange peel

Preheat oven to 400°. Grease muffin tins.

In small bowl, combine blueberries and 2 tsp flour; set aside.

In another small bowl, combine eggs, oil, orange juice, and peel; set aside.

In large bowl, combine 1-3/4 cup flour, baking powder, nutmeg, and cinnamon. Add egg mixture to dry ingredients. Stir gently but do not over stir. Fold in blucberries.

Fill muffin tins about 2/3 full and bake 20 to 25 minutes.

The Staff of Life

"Bread deals with living things, with giving life,
with growth, with the seed, the grain that nurtures.
It is not coincidence that we say
bread is the staff of life."

Lionel Poilane

BLUEBERRY SCONES

2 cups whole wheat flour, sifted
   Dash of salt
1/4 tsp baking soda
1/2 tsp cinnamon
   2 tsp baking powder (See page 143)
1/4 cup butter
   1 cup blueberries
   1 Tbsp honey
   1 Tbsp unsulphured molasses
3/4 cup buttermilk

Mix dry ingredients together. With pastry blender, cut in butter. Gently mix blueberries into dry mixture. Stir in honey and molasses, then buttermilk. Gently form into a ball.

Transfer dough to a floured surface and pat to about 1/2-inch thickness. With a spatula, divide the dough into eight triangles. Place scones on a greased cookie sheet and bake at 425° for 12 to 15 minutes.

These are delicious served hot with butter. They can be served as breakfast, dessert, or a snack.

~ To make chocolate chip scones, simply use 1 cup chocolate chips in place of the blueberries. Or, to make blueberry-chocolate chip scones, use 3/4 cup blueberries and 1/2 cup chocolate chips.

~ When making scones, it is easier to work with blueberries if they are frozen, rather than fresh.

~ Speaking of frozen blueberries, they make delightful snacks. Pop them from the freezer to your mouth for a burst of flavor! Do not rinse blueberries prior to freezing.

BUTTERMILK BISCUITS

2 cups whole wheat flour
1/2 tsp sea salt
1 tsp baking soda
1/2 cup butter
1 cup buttermilk

Note: It is *very* important that you use *finely* ground whole wheat flour.

Mix together whole wheat flour, salt, and baking soda. Cut in butter. Add buttermilk. Mix well, but do not over mix.

Pat into 3/4-inch thickness on floured surface. Cut biscuits and if desired, brush with melted butter.

Bake at 425° for 15 to 20 minutes.

The Sweet Side

In our home, the preferred sweetener is raw honey. As a result, we use raw honey in many of our recipes. Bill finds that, even when it is used to sweeten baked goods, his digestive system tolerates it better than many other sweeteners.

Experiment with the wide array of natural sweeteners to find what suits your health needs and taste buds.

Keep in mind, however, that even natural sweeteners should be used moderately. (Processed sweeteners should not be used at all.) As a society, we are overly fond of sweets. Generally, a little is okay; a lot is not.

CINNAMON ROLLS*

Step 1
Follow Steps 1-6 of the Whole Wheat Bread recipe on page 73. Form two loaves, rather than four, to make Whole Wheat Bread. Proceed with Whole Wheat Bread recipe. Use remaining dough to make cinnamon rolls.

Step 2
With rolling pin, roll remaining dough out onto generously floured surface, shaping into a large rectangle as you roll. Dough will be very stretchy at first, but as you keep forcing the dough with the rolling pin, it will eventually give way. Keep surface well floured.

Step 3
When dough is rolled out to approximately 1/3 inch thickness, spread *about 1 cup softened butter (no substitutes)* generously over entire surface of the dough.

Step 4
Then, generously sprinkle dough with *about 2 cups turbinado (raw) sugar* and *about 1/2 cup cinnamon.*

Step 5
Roll up the dough, spreading a little more butter on the back side. When completely rolled up, pinch in sides. Using a serrated knife, cut dough every 1-1/2 inches.

Step 6
Place cinnamon rolls spiral side down in 9 x 13-inch buttered pan. (Generally, 15 cinnamon rolls can fit into one pan.)

Step 7
Let cinnamon rolls rise about an hour.

Step 8
Bake in 350° oven for about 30 minutes.

CINNAMON ROLLS (Cont.)

Step 9
Let set about 10 to 15 minutes before serving. These taste best when served right away. If you have leftover cinnamon rolls, do not cover them tightly when storing them; they will become mushy. Rather, simply cover with a clean dish towel.

Makes at least 2 dozen (yummy) cinnamon rolls

* Recipe Contributed by Melanie Chandler

Making a Home

Women set the atmosphere of their homes. They are "homemakers." Even if they must also work outside the home, the home is still their world.

Far more important than keeping a house clean and neat, the homemaker should maintain a peaceful and loving attitude. When her relationship with God is pure and good, she will naturally exude peace and kindness to others.

Her attitude – not expensive furnishings and state-of-the-art appliances – is what will make her home a haven for her family, friends, and visitors. People will look forward to returning to this pleasant environment, where they can be refreshed and nurtured – physically, emotionally, and spiritually.

"She openeth her mouth with wisdom; and in her tongue is the law of kindness."
Proverbs 31:26

LEMON POPPY SEED MUFFINS

1-1/4 cups whole wheat flour
1/2 tsp baking soda
1/2 tsp baking powder (See page 143)
1/4 tsp salt
2 large egg whites
1/2 cup plain yogurt
1/2 cup unsweetened applesauce
1/3 cup honey
1/3 cup fresh squeezed lemon juice
1 tsp pure lemon extract
2 Tbsp poppy seeds

Preheat oven to 375°.

Mix and double sift flour, baking soda, baking powder and salt; set aside.

In medium bowl, add egg whites, yogurt, applesauce, honey, lemon juice and lemon extract. Whisk until well blended. Mix in poppy seeds.

Add flour mixture to egg white mixture and mix just till moistened. Be careful to not over mix.

Evenly distribute batter between 12 regular sized greased muffin tins, filling 2/3 full. Bake for 25 minutes or till inserted toothpick comes out clean.

Makes 12 muffins

Egg Whites

When beating eggs whites, add a pinch of salt.
They will beat faster and higher.

WHOLE WHEAT BREAD*

Step 1
In a small bowl or glass measuring cup, whisk together *1 cup lukewarm water* and *3 very rounded tablespoons yeast* until yeast is dissolved; set aside.

Step 2
Place the following ingredients in a very large bowl:
5 cups lukewarm water
3 Tbsp salt
1/2 cup butter (no substitutes)
1 cup honey or maple syrup
6 cups freshly ground white wheat flour

Step 3
Whisk together the flour mixture until well blended and no longer clumpy. Add yeast mixture. Continue mixing until well blended.

Step 4
Gradually add more flour, mixing after each flour addition, until stiff, yet sticky dough is formed. (Note: You will use almost 5 pounds of flour for this entire recipe.)

Step 5
When stiff, yet sticky dough is formed, turn it out onto a well floured surface. Knead the dough until it is smooth and elastic and no longer sticky. At this point the dough should be firm. Kneading should take about 10 to 15 minutes. During this kneading process, be sure to keep the surface well floured.

Step 6
Place dough in oiled bowl and let rise until double in size. This can take anywhere from one to two hours, depending on the climate and temperature of your home. When dough is double in size, punch it down.

WHOLE WHEAT BREAD (Cont.)

Step 7
Divide and shape dough into four loaves.

Step 8
Oil four bread pans (unless they are nonstick bread pans). Place shaped bread into bread pans. Let rise until about double in size again. This second rising will take about an hour.

Step 9
Bake in 350° oven for about 40 minutes. Remove pans from oven and let set for 5 to 10 minutes. Remove bread from pans and set on wooden bread boards or wire racks to cool completely.

Step 10
Store in plastic bags. Freeze bread that will not be used within a week. Bread may be frozen for several weeks.

Makes 4 loaves of bread

~ See Cinnamon Rolls recipe on page 70 to make both whole wheat bread and cinnamon rolls using this recipe.

~ Do not be alarmed by the word "white" in the phrase "white wheat flour." This is not bleached, refined white flour. It is flour that is naturally whiter than other varieties of whole wheat flour. Milled from hard spring wheat, white wheat flour is preferred by some bakers who value it for its mild taste, light color, and baking properties which closely mirror refined white flour.

~ If you have a grain mill, Melanie recommends that you buy "hard spring wheat" grains to make your own white wheat flour. If you do not have a grain mill, you can purchase white wheat flour.

* Recipe Contributed by Melanie Chandler

WHOLE WHEAT BREAD WITH FRESH HERBS

1-1/2 cups finely ground whole wheat flour
   1 Tbsp gluten
   1/2 cup rolled oats (not quick-cooking or instant)
   1/2 tsp baking soda
   1/2 tsp sea salt
   1/4 tsp freshly ground pepper
   1/4 cup chopped scallions (green part only)
   1/4 cup chopped fresh parsley
     2 Tbsp chopped fresh basil
     2 large eggs
     1 cup buttermilk
     1 Tbsp extra virgin olive oil

Preheat oven to 375°. Coat a 9 x 5-inch loaf pan with cooking oil. In large bowl, combine flour, gluten, oats, baking soda, salt, and pepper. Mix in scallions, parsley, and basil. Set aside.

In small bowl, lightly beat eggs. Add buttermilk and oil; mix well. Add to flour mixture. Mix just until combined.

Pour batter into prepared pan. Bake about 45 minutes, until knife inserted in center comes out clean. Cool in pan 10 minutes. Remove from pan and cool completely on wire rack.

Makes 10 slices

~ This bread is great eaten hot with butter. Also, it makes a wonderful appetizer when sliced and dipped in olive oil with freshly grated Parmesan cheese and fresh cracked black pepper.

~ If you do not have gluten, use 1/2 cup whole wheat bread flour and 1 cup whole wheat flour.

WHOLE WHEAT PUMPKIN MUFFINS

1-1/4 cups honey
1/2 cup vegetable oil
3 eggs
1-1/2 cups pumpkin
1/2 cup water
3 cups whole wheat flour
1-1/2 tsp baking powder (See page 143)
1 tsp baking soda
1 tsp sea salt
1/2 tsp cloves
3/4 tsp cinnamon
1 tsp nutmeg
1-1/2 Tbsp ground flaxseeds, optional
1 cup walnuts
1 cup raisins, optional

In a large bowl, mix together honey, oil, eggs, pumpkin, and water.

In a small bowl, mix together flour, baking powder, baking soda, salt, spices, and flaxseeds. Add to first mixture and blend together with electric mixer. Add walnuts and raisins, if desired. Let stand one hour at room temperature.

Grease muffin tins and fill them 3/4 of the way. Bake 15 minutes at 400°.

Makes 2 dozen muffins

~ These muffins freeze well for future use.

~ This recipe has special meaning to us. We started making these back when we were first experimenting with healthier cooking and baking techniques. We liked them then and we like them now. They are one of the recipes that have survived our many experiments!

ZUCCHINI BREAD

1-1/2 cups whole wheat flour
   1 tsp ground cinnamon
1/2 tsp baking soda
1/4 tsp baking powder (See page 143)
1/4 tsp sea salt
1/4 tsp ground nutmeg
1/4 tsp ground ginger
3/4 cup honey
   1 cup finely shredded unpeeled zucchini
1/4 cup cooking oil
3/4 tsp vanilla
   1 egg
1/4 tsp finely shredded lemon peel
1/2 cup chopped walnuts, optional

In a small mixing bowl combine flour, cinnamon, baking soda, baking powder, salt, nutmeg, and ginger.

In a larger bowl combine honey, zucchini, oil, vanilla, egg, and lemon peel. Add flour mixture and stir together. Stir in walnuts, if desired.

Pour batter into greased 8 x 4 x 2-inch glass or stoneware loaf pan. Bake at 350° for about 50 minutes, or until toothpick inserted in the center comes out clean. Place pan on wire rack for 10 minutes, then remove bread from pan and cool thoroughly on a wire rack; wrap.

Store overnight before slicing and serving. (The flavor of the bread is better after it has set a while.)

Makes 1 loaf

~ Bill thinks this zucchini bread is the best he has ever had. (Of course, he might be just a little biased to my baking!) Try it yourself and see if you agree.

$ Money Saving Tip $

Why does healthy food cost so much?

On the surface, healthy food seems to cost more than less healthy options. The simple reason is this: It costs more because *it's worth more.*

When considering purchasing a healthy item, we usually ask "How much does this cost?" We also need to ask "How much is this worth?" Look beyond the visible price tag.

In the long run, healthy food and quality kitchen equipment is worth a lot more than its price, even if it seems expensive initially. You are likely to save money from days missed from work due to sickness. You might save when you don't have to buy your children allergy, cough, and cold medicine. It is possible that you might even save by avoiding serious, debilitating sicknesses and diseases. We must learn to look beyond the here-and-now to the effect our present choices will have on our futures.

Higher quality products have more nutrition. They are foods which enhance your health instead of detract from your health. That in itself is worth a lot! In reality, you get more bang for your buck.

PASTA

CHICKEN FETTUCCINE ALFREDO

8-oz fettuccine noodles (We recommend
    Ezekiel 4:9 Sprouted Grain Pasta noodles.)
3 Tbsp oil
3 cloves garlic, chopped fine
1/2 cup thinly sliced onions
2 cups heavy cream
1 tsp Organic Better than Bouillon Chicken Base
1/4 cup sundried tomatoes, thinly sliced
1/2 cup grilled chicken breasts, thinly sliced
1 cup Parmesan cheese, freshly grated

Cook noodles according to package directions. (To keep pasta from sticking together, do *not* add oil to pasta while boiling. If oil sticks to pasta, sauce won't. Do not drop pasta in all at once; rather, let it slip through your fingers into the pot a little at a time while turning your hand in a circular motion, then stir gently and move pasta around.) Rinse in cool water; drain. Set aside.

To infuse garlic into oil, simmer garlic in oil for a few minutes. Stir in onions; simmer, covered, till translucent, about 15 minutes; stir occasionally. Turn up heat to medium-high and add cream, Better than Bouillon Chicken Base, sundried tomatoes, and chicken; stir often. Cook till sauce begins to thicken.

Add noodles; cook till sauce reaches desired thickness. Serve immediately, generously sprinkling each portion of alfredo with Parmesan cheese and a pinch of nutmeg.

Poetic Moment

Whether small or large, wide or thin,
Keep pasta handy in the pasta bin.

Choose whole grain pasta, it's the best.
Healthy enough to be worth the quest.

PESTO TORTELLINI

9 oz (about 2 cups) cheese tortellini noodles
1/4 cup scallions, white and light green parts, sliced
1/4 cup sundried tomatoes, diced small
1 Tbsp pine nuts
3 Tbsp pesto
1/4 cup fresh, grated Parmesan cheese

Cook noodles according to package directions; drain. Rinse with cold water and drain again. Place in a medium bowl and toss with all other ingredients.

Serve warm as an entrée or side dish. Or, refrigerate and serve as a cold pasta salad. (We prefer it as a pasta salad.)

~ Tortellini is available with many deliciously flavored fillings, such as different cheeses, spinach, and sun dried tomato.

~ This is one of Sylvia's favorite recipes.

Al dente

Al dente is an Italian term used to describe perfectly cooked noodles. These noodles are neither too hard (undercooked) nor too soft (overcooked). Al dente pasta is firm but not hard.

As your pasta is cooking, taste it. When it reaches a point of firm chewiness, it is al dentc.

SOBA NOODLES WITH PEANUT SAUCE

1 lb soba noodles
4 cloves garlic, minced
2 Tbsp peeled, grated fresh ginger root
4 green onions, chopped
  (Use the white and pale green parts.)
4 Tbsp unsalted, fresh ground peanut butter
1 Tbsp tahini (ground sesame seeds)
4 tsp tamari or shoyu soy sauce
4 Tbsp rice vinegar
2 Tbsp sesame seeds, toasted
1/2 cup hot water

Cook noodles according to package directions. Drain, rinse under cold running water, and drain again. Set aside.

In a food processor or blender, combine all ingredients except noodles and process until smooth. Put this sauce in a large bowl. Transfer the noodles to the bowl and toss to coat.

Cover and refrigerate until thoroughly chilled, at least three hours. Toss again before serving.

Serves 4

~ Don't be hesitant to try this recipe just because the ingredients may be unfamiliar to you. This is a light, quick, fun dish with a unique, pleasant flavor.

~ Soba noodles are made of buckwheat. They are a Japanese favorite.

VEGETABLE LASAGNA*

Note: To be sure you have all the ingredients you need and to familiarize yourself with procedure for making this lasagna, read all directions before you begin.

Step 1 - Noodles
Cook 16 lasagna noodles according to package directions, about 10 to 12 minutes. Drain and rinse with cold water; set aside.

Step 2 - Sauce
2 28-oz cans crushed tomatoes
1 Tbsp oregano
1 Tbsp basil
1 small pinch crushed red pepper
3 cloves garlic
Place sauce ingredients in a pot and simmer.
While sauce is simmering, prepare cheese mixture and sauté the vegetables.

Step 3 - Cheese Mixture
2 beaten eggs
32 oz cottage cheese
16 oz mozzarella cheese
3 oz Parmesan cheese
Milk
Combine eggs, and three cheeses. Add just enough milk to make it spreadable.
(In addition to the above, set aside an *8 oz mixture of mozzarella and Parmesan cheeses* to put on the top before baking.)

Step 4 - Vegetables
2 Tbsp olive oil
1 medium onion, chopped
1 cup chopped carrots
1 cup chopped squash and/or zucchini
1/2 cup mushrooms, chopped
2 cups fresh spinach or 1 cup frozen spinach

VEGETABLE LASAGNA (Cont.)

Sauté onions, carrots, and squash in oil for about 5 minutes. Add mushrooms and cook just until tender. Add spinach and cook for about a minute.

Step 5 – Layering and Baking
Put a thin layer of sauce in a 9 x 13-inch baking dish. Add a layer of noodles, and then add vegetables. Spread cheese mixture over the veggies, and then add sauce. Repeat the layers so you end up with noodles on the top. Add a thin layer of sauce, and then sprinkle mixture of mozzarella and Parmesan cheeses. Bake in a 350° oven for about 35 minutes.

* Recipe Contributed by Michelle Schrift

Eat to your Heart's Content

It is satisfying to eat food that tastes good and makes you feel good too. When you're done eating, you think, *I've done something good for my temple.* That's better than thinking, *I wish I wouldn't have eaten that. Now I feel horrible.*

The taste of healthy food "grows on you." Though the taste of a food may be unfamiliar, before long I usually find myself saying, "Hey, this tastes really good. I think I like it."

We often hear people say, "Nothing that tastes good is good for me." However, we believe that whole foods taste great. In fact, once you wean yourself away from chemical laden, artificially flavored, colored, manufactured foods, your taste buds will be revitalized with new awareness of the delicious flavors of real foods.

VEGETABLES

BALSAMIC VEGETABLE SANDWICHES

2 red bell peppers, sliced 3/8-inch thick
1/4 cup balsamic vinegar
1 Tbsp butter
2 medium yellow onions, sliced 1/8-inch thick
4 portabella mushroom caps, sliced 3/8-inch thick
8 servings ciabatta bread, organic if possible
1 lb asiago cheese, sliced

Step One
In a medium bowl, marinate peppers in balsamic vinegar for 30 minutes, stirring occasionally.

Step Two
In large skillet, melt 1/2 tablespoon butter on low to medium heat. Transfer bell peppers to skillet; set aside balsamic vinegar. Cover bell peppers and cook at a low simmer for 15 minutes, stirring occasionally.

Step Three
Stir in half of retained balsamic vinegar. Turn heat to medium-high and cook, covered, five more minutes.

Step Four
Just before removing bell peppers from pan, add remaining balsamic vinegar. Peppers will be ready to remove when balsamic vinegar has evaporated and edges of peppers have browned.

Step Five
In clean pan, melt 1/2 tablespoon butter. Add onions and cook at low-medium heat, covered, for 15 minutes. Add mushrooms; cook at medium to medium-high heat for additional 5 minutes.

Step Six
Preheat oven to 325°.

BALSAMIC VEGETABLE SANDWICHES (Cont.)

Step Seven
For each sandwich, place one ounce of cheese on the bottom half of bread. Then layer mushrooms, onions, and bell peppers. Place another ounce of cheese on top of vegetables. Place top half of bread on vegetables.

Step Eight
Lightly wrap sandwiches separately in aluminum foil and place on a baking sheet. Bake 12 minutes.

Makes 8 sandwiches

~ Cooked vegetables may be stored in refrigerator up to three days if necessary.

Sautéing

Sautéed foods are cooked quickly, in a small amount of oil, over medium-high to high heat. Foods like fish, vegetables, and tender meat are uniformly cut into thin pieces.

In French, "sauté" means "to jump." This refers to the necessity of quickly tossing ingredients around the pan, till tender and lightly browned. A sauté pan must be large enough to easily hold all the food in one layer, so steam can escape. The simple technique of sautéing maximizes flavor while minimizing cooking time.

Pan frying is different from sautéing. Pan frying uses thicker pieces of food, does not require as high heat, and food is not turned as often.

CHEESE AND TOMATO TART

1 9-inch pie crust (See page 158)
1/4 cup fresh basil leaves, chopped
or 4 tsp ground basil
1/2 cup ricotta cheese
2 large eggs, slightly beaten
1/4 lb grated mozzarella cheese
1/2 cup grated Parmesan cheese
4 or 5 (about 2 lbs) ripe tomatoes,
sliced 1/4-inch thick
Extra virgin olive oil

Bake crust until barely done. While crust is baking, combine chopped basil and ricotta. Add eggs and mix until well combined. Add the mozzarella and Parmesan cheeses. Spread the mixture into the baked crust.

Arrange tomatoes over the cheese mixture. Drizzle with olive oil. Cover and bake in a 350° oven for 40 to 50 minutes. Cool for 10 minutes before serving.

Serves 6

Simply Fresh

"You don't have to cook fancy or complicated masterpieces – just good food from fresh ingredients."

Julia Child

CREAMY CUCUMBERS

1/2 cup plain yogurt or sour cream
    Dash of cayenne pepper
1/4 tsp dried dill
  1 tsp sea salt
  1 tsp raw honey
  1 tsp lemon juice or apple cider vinegar
  1 large cucumber, halved lengthwise, seeded,
    and thinly sliced (about three cups)
  1 small onion, thinly sliced

Stir together yogurt or sour cream, seasonings, honey, and lemon juice or vinegar. Add cucumber and onion. Toss to coat.

Before serving, cover and chill for at least two hours, stirring often.

~ Creamy Cucumbers get watery if kept for too long without eating. Prepare and serve them the same day.

~ These may be used as a side dish, salad, or snack.

~ Sometimes cucumber skins can be tough. If that is the case with the cucumbers you are using, peel the skins first. However, if your cucumbers are organic, it is better to leave the skins on.

Humility is Healthy

"In the course of my life, I have often had to eat my words, and I must confess that I have always found it a wholesome diet."

Winston Churchill

GREEN BEANS WITH TOMATOES

2 Tbsp olive oil
2 cloves garlic, minced
1 lb (2 cups) fresh green beans, trimmed
    Salt and pepper, to taste
1 large tomato, peeled and diced small
1 cup fresh basil leaves, minced
2 to 4 oz feta cheese, crumbled
    Pine nuts, if desired

In large sauté pan, heat olive oil over medium heat until hot. Add garlic and sauté until golden. Add green beans and sprinkle with salt and pepper. Once beans are hot, add a little water to the pan; cover. Cook, stirring occasionally, until green beans are almost tender but still firm. (If necessary, continue to add small amounts of water to keep beans from drying out.)

Add tomato and basil, turn up heat and cook about 5 minutes, stirring frequently.

Transfer bean mixture to a serving bowl and sprinkle with feta cheese and, if desired, pine nuts.

Serves 6

~ This is especially delicious in the summer, when green beans, tomatoes, and basil are fresh from the garden. Yum!!!

Steamed Vegetables

Steaming is probably the healthiest way to cook vegetables. (It is also fast and easy.) Vegetables are cooked over hot water, keeping food moist. Unlike frying, microwaving, and boiling, steaming retains most of the flavor and nutrition of the vegetables.

NEW POTATOES
WITH BUTTER-PARSLEY SAUCE

        2 lb small new potatoes, unpeeled
1-1/2 cups butter
        8 cloves garlic, minced
        2 tsp sea salt
        2 tsp fresh ground black pepper
        1 cup fresh parsley, snipped

Cook potatoes in boiling water until tender, about 25 minutes; drain water from pot.

While potatoes are cooking, melt butter in small saucepan on low heat. Add garlic, salt, pepper, and parsley and simmer 5 minutes. When potatoes have been drained, halve or quarter potatoes. Mix butter mixture into potatoes. Heat on low for several minutes and serve.

~ I don't think anyone could deny that these potatoes are fantastic.

The Spice of Life

If you are a person that uses the same few spices over and over or if you don't use any spices at all, venture beyond your comfort zone. Fresh and dried spices and herbs add flavor and nutrition to food. They will open up a delicious new world to you and enhance your cooking and baking.

When using dried spices, rubbing them between your fingers before adding them to food will help release the flavors.

PARMESAN POTATOES AND ONIONS

2 lb potatoes, thinly sliced
1 medium onion, thinly sliced
3 Tbsp olive oil
4 Tbsp Parmesan cheese
2 tsp paprika

Preheat oven to 400°.

In a large bowl, toss together potatoes, onion, and olive oil. Spread on a large baking sheet with sides. During baking, turn potatoes and onions several times. Bake until potatoes and onions are golden brown and cooked through, about 45 minutes.

A few minutes before potatoes are done, sprinkle cheese and paprika over them. When cheese is melted, remove potatoes from oven and serve immediately. Season with sea salt.

Parmesan Cheese

True Italian Parmesan cheese is a world apart from the typical American-style Parmesan most people buy to sprinkle on their spaghetti. There is no comparison in flavor and quality.

Its Italian name is Parmigiano Reggiano. We buy blocks of raw milk Parmigiano Reggiano and grate it ourselves. Because of its superb flavor, a little goes a long way; so it is an economical purchase.

Give it a try. You might decide to use this flavorful cheese exclusively!

PORTOBELLO MUSHROOMS WITH SPINACH-CHEESE FILLING

2 to 4 Portobello mushrooms, depending on size
      (1 to 2 per person)
  2 tsp olive oil
1/3 lb (about 3 cups) raw spinach
1/3 cup grated Gruyere, Swiss, or cheddar cheese
      (We use Gruyere.)
  1 tsp freshly grated Romano cheese
     Small dash freshly ground black pepper
     Small dash hot sauce (such as Tabasco)
       or a pinch of cayenne pepper
     Toasted pine nuts, for garnish

Step One
Remove and discard mushroom stems and gills. Wipe mushroom caps with a damp cloth to clean.

Step Two
In a skillet, sauté mushrooms in olive oil until barely tender and juicy. (Don't cook them all the way through; they will soon be baked.) Transfer to a lightly oiled baking dish.

Step Three
Steam spinach until just wilted, about 5 minutes. Place wilted spinach in a colander and spray with cold water. Squeeze out excess moisture and chop.

Step Four
Stir together chopped spinach, grated cheeses, black pepper, and hot sauce or cayenne pepper. Set aside.

Step Five
Prepare Mornay sauce.

Step Six
Add spinach-cheese mixture to Mornay sauce. Fill each mushroom with mixture.

PORTOBELLO MUSHROOMS WITH SPINACH-CHEESE FILLING (Cont.)

Step Seven
Bake mushrooms, uncovered, at 350° for 15 to 20 minutes or till filling is bubbling and lightly browned.

Step Eight
Garnish with pine nuts and serve.

Serves 2

~ These mushrooms are not only scrumptious; they are beautiful to look at...definitely not your run-of-the-mill side dish!

Mornay Sauce

1/2 cup milk
  1 Tbsp melted butter
  2 tsp unbleached flour
1/3 cup grated Gruyere or Swiss cheese
   Small pinch of grated nutmeg
   Small pinch of ground coriander
   Salt and pepper, to taste

Heat milk to steaming; set aside.

Melt butter in a saucepan. Add flour; stir to make a thick paste. Rapidly whisk in steaming milk. Heat until thickened, whisking briskly and constantly to prevent lumps. Gently whisk in grated cheese and seasonings.

~ Mornay sauce is a Béchamel sauce with the addition of cheese. Gruyère is most commonly used to make Mornay sauce, although Swiss is good as well. Mornay sauce can be served with fish, eggs and vegetables.

POTATO CASSEROLE

10 cups frozen hash browns
1/4 cup plus 2 Tbsp melted butter
1 can organic cream of chicken soup
12 oz sour cream
1/2 cup milk
1/2 cup chopped green onions
2 cups grated sharp or extra sharp cheddar cheese

Preheat oven to 375°.

Pour 1/4 cup melted butter into 9 x 13-inch baking dish. Add 5 cups frozen hash browns.

In bowl, mix soup, sour cream, milk, and green onions.

Pour 1/2 soup mixture over hash browns. Sprinkle 1 cup grated cheese on top. Add remainder of hash browns, then soup mixture on top. Sprinkle on remaining cheese. Drizzle 2 tablespoons melted butter on top.

Bake for 50 to 60 minutes.

The Other Potato

Sweet potatoes are often overlooked in favor of the common potato. This should not be, since they are an excellent source of vitamin A, high in vitamin C and manganese, and good sources of vitamin B6, dietary fiber, potassium, iron, and copper.

Sweet potatoes don't need much help;
they are delicious all by themselves.
Try them baked or cooked over an open fire.

PUMPKIN CASSEROLE

1 30-oz can organic unsweetened pumpkin
2 apples, peeled and chopped
1/2 cup raisins, if desired
2 tsp cinnamon
1/4 tsp nutmeg
2 Tbsp molasses
1/2 cup chopped walnuts

Preheat oven to 375°.

Mix together all ingredients and pour into a lightly oiled loaf pan. Bake for 20 minutes. Serve hot.

Serves 4 to 6

The Milky Way

Some people think we are crazy, but we have drunk raw cow, goat, sheep...even camel milk. (The camel milk was the most interesting. We watched a Bedouin man milk the camels. He then gave us that milk. For sure, it was fresh!) We have found all this milk delicious. In North America, of course cow milk is most common.

We do our very best to ensure that the raw milk we consume is safe to drink. Many times we go to the dairy farm to look at the cows and ask the dairyman pertinent questions about the animals' feed and treatment. Almost always, we buy milk that is certified organic. This milk is routinely inspected and meets or exceeds stringent regulations. In addition to providing us with a nutritious food, our precautions help ensure that our raw milk is safe and clean.

ROASTED BUTTERNUT SQUASH

1 butternut squash, peeled, seeded, and uniformly
    chopped into 1-inch chunks
1/2 cup dried, sweetened cranberries
2 cups coarsely chopped onions
1/4 tsp ground cloves
1/2 tsp ground black pepper
    1 tsp ground cinnamon
    1 tsp ground nutmeg
    2 Tbsp coarsely chopped fresh sage
    2 Tbsp melted butter

Preheat oven to 350°.

Combine all ingredients in a 9 x 13-inch baking dish.

Cover and bake 45 minutes, stirring occasionally.
Remove cover and roast for an additional 15 minutes.

Sick with Worry?

Do you worry a lot? Do you get easily agitated
when things don't go your way? Do you feel
distressed over circumstances in your life?

Anxiety, worry, and fear contribute to poor
health. There is a solution so simple that some
people doubt it works. The secret is complete
dependence on God, acknowledging our
limitations as we cast our cares on Him, because
He cares for us (I Peter 5:7). Isaiah 26:3-4 says
"Thou wilt keep him in perfect peace, whose mind
is stayed on thee: because he trusteth in thee.
Trust ye in the LORD for ever: for in the LORD
JEHOVAH is everlasting strength."

SIMPLE CARROTS

2 Tbsp butter
4 carrots, sliced into 1/4-inch rounds

Steam or lightly boil carrots until tender but still crisp. Drain water. Stir in butter until melted.

Transfer carrots to serving dish. Sprinkle with sesame seeds or fresh, snipped parsley.

~ Once you learn to enjoy the naturally sweet flavor of simply cooked carrots, you'll probably never again eat overcooked, marshmallow-smothered carrots!

$ Money Saving Tip $

Eat at home more often.

If you eat out a lot, cut back on your restaurant visits. You can buy a lot of good groceries for the price of a meal or two eaten out.

Many people say they eat out a lot because they don't have time to cook. In the same time it takes to get seated at a restaurant, order your food, eat, and pay the bill, you could be preparing and eating home cooked food.

The "I don't have time to cook" phrase is invalid since it often takes just as much time to eat out at a sit-down restaurant as it does to cook a nourishing meal.

SPANAKOPITA

        1 lb organic whole wheat or spelt fillo dough
1-1/2 cups chopped onions
        1 bunch scallions, white and green parts, chopped
        2 lb frozen cut organic spinach
        1 lb cottage cheese
1-1/2 lb feta cheese
        3 large eggs
        2 Tbsp olive oil
        3 sticks unsalted butter, melted

Step One
Before beginning, make sure spinach is thawed. Also, unopened package of fillo dough must be thawed in refrigerator 7 to 8 hours, then allowed to stand at room temperature 2 hours.

Step Two
On low to medium heat, cook onions and scallions in a small amount of butter until soft; set aside.

Step Three
Squeeze spinach to remove as much excess water as possible. Then place spinach between paper towels and press to further dry.

Step Four
In a large bowl, use your hands to combine onions, scallions, spinach, cottage cheese, feta cheese, eggs, and olive oil. Mix very well.

Step Five
Use a pastry brush to brush butter on bottom and sides of pan(s). (Use either one 13 x 18-inch pan or two 9 x 13-inch pans. If using two 9 x 13-inch pans, cut the fillo dough in half before continuing with recipe.)

SPANAKOPITA (Cont.)

Step Six
Place 1 sheet of fillo dough in pan at a time and brush with butter. Continue layering and buttering until you have used 9 sheets.

Step Seven
Spread spinach mixture evenly over fillo dough. (If using two pans, use half of the spinach mixture in each pan.)

Step Eight
Repeat Step Six until 9 more layers have been added on top of spinach mixture. Butter top layer of fillo dough. (Note: You might not need to use all the butter.)

Step Nine
With a sharp knife, score the top layers of fillo dough, making 24 pieces of spanakopita.

Step Ten
Bake in a preheated 350° oven for 50 to 60 minutes, until light golden brown.

Step Eleven
Allow spanakopita to stand for at least 15 minutes. Following scored lines, cut individual pieces.

~ Fillo dough is delicate. Work with it gently and patiently.

~ Place moist paper towels on top of the stack(s) of fillo dough. This will keep the fillo dough from drying out while you are layering and buttering.

~ Spanakopita, which means "spinach pie," is a traditional Greek favorite. There's nothing else quite like it...and it is fun to prepare.

STUFFED ACORN SQUASH

  1 acorn squash
  2 Granny Smith apples, peeled, cored, and cubed
1-1/2 Tbsp (or more) butter
  3 Tbsp maple syrup
  1 tsp cinnamon
    Salt

Cut acorn squash in half widthwise. Remove and discard pulp and seeds.

Pour a small amount of water in a baking dish. Place squash, cut side down, in dish. Bake at 350° for 30 minutes.

Remove squash from dish and allow to cool slightly. Remove squash meat from rind. Discard rind and place meat in small casserole dish.

Add apples, butter, maple syrup, cinnamon, and salt. Mix together.

Cover dish and bake 30 to 45 minutes, or until squash and apples are tender.

Vegetable Wraps

For a quick and healthy lunch, wrap grilled vegetables in whole grain tortillas. You can add other ingredients – such as beans or rice – but the grilled vegetables are good all by themselves.
Try tortillas made from spelt or brown rice.
You can grill the vegetables and refrigerate them until you are ready to make your wraps.
They reheat quickly.

SWEET POTATO CASSEROLE

    4 cups sweet potatoes, peeled and cubed
    4 Tbsp butter, softened
1-1/2 tsp vanilla
    1/4 cup maple syrup
    1/4 cup barley malt syrup
    3/4 tsp ground ginger
        1 tsp ground cinnamon
        1 tsp salt
        2 eggs, beaten
    1/4 cup milk
        1 cup pecans, chopped
        1 Granny Smith apple, peeled and cut into
            1/2-inch cubes
    1/4 cup raisins, optional

Boil potatoes. When soft, drain and mash with a fork.

Add butter, vanilla, maple syrup, and barley malt syrup; mix together. Add ginger, cinnamon, and salt. Stir in eggs, then milk. Add pecans, apples, and raisins.

Transfer mixture to an 8 x 8-inch baking dish. Bake at 350° for 30 to 40 minutes.

Rice Cooking Tips

Refrain from stirring rice while it is cooking and your rice will not become gummy and sticky.

Also, when rice is done, remove rice pot from heat and remove the lid. Let rice stand for 10 to 15 minutes. Then, do not stir rice with a spoon; rather, fluff it with a fork.

THAI VEGETABLE STIR FRY

4 cups cooked brown rice
1 cup organic chicken broth
1 tsp Organic Better than Bouillon Chicken Base
3 Tbsp fish sauce
1-1/2 Tbsp fermented soy sauce
     (Use less if not using fermented soy sauce.)
2 tsp black pepper
1 Tbsp honey
1/2 Tbsp molasses
1-1/2 Tbsp olive oil
5 garlic cloves, chopped
2 cups yellow onions, sliced
1/2 each medium green, red, yellow, and orange bell
     peppers, sliced into strips
1 cup carrots, sliced 1/4-inch thick
2 cups broccoli florets
1 cup zucchini, sliced 1/8-inch thick
2-1/2 cups baby bella mushrooms, cut in strips
     approximately 1/8-inch thick
1 cup fresh chopped basil
6 oz pea pods
1/2 bunch green onions, including tops, chopped
1-1/2 cup dry roasted cashews

Step One
Cook brown rice according to directions. (Do not stir while cooking.) Make sure rice is almost done before cooking vegetables.

Step Two
Total cook time for vegetables is approximately 10 minutes. Make sure all ingredients are cut up before starting to cook vegetables. This will aid the cooking process and keep vegetables crisp.

THAI VEGETABLE STIR FRY (Cont.)

Step Three
In a small saucepan, mix chicken broth, Better than Bouillon Chicken Base, fish sauce, soy sauce, pepper, honey and molasses. Cover and bring to a simmer about 5 minutes before cooking vegetables, stirring frequently.

Step Four
Begin heating large wok, large skillet or frying pan and pour in olive oil and garlic. Simmer for one minute and add yellow onions and bell peppers; continue to simmer, covered, for 2 minutes, stirring once a minute.

Step Five
Add 1/2 the sauce, turn to high heat and bring to a boil quickly. Add carrots. Cook for 1 minute, uncovered, and continue stirring frequently throughout remainder of process.

Step Six
Add remainder of sauce, bring back to boil and add broccoli, zucchini, mushrooms, and chopped basil. Cook, uncovered, two minutes.

Step Seven
Add pea pods and 1/2 of the green onions; cook two minutes.

Step Eight
Serve immediately over rice. Sprinkle with cashews and remaining green onions.

Serves 4

~ This dish is a medley of fresh vegetables with a distinctive Asian flair. It is exceptionally delicious and a bit spicy.

~ You may also use water chestnuts, bamboo shoots, bean sprouts (thick white sprouts), or sesame seeds.

FISH

CUCUMBER DILL SAUCE

1 cup peeled, seeded, and minced cucumbers
1 cup mayonnaise (See page 191)
3 Tbsp finely chopped fresh dill
4 tsp raw honey

Place minced cucumber in sieve; use spoon to press out excess water.

Mix together all ingredients. Before serving, chill for several hours.

~ This sauce is especially good with trout but can also be served with other types of fish.

Piles of Smiles

A man from Europe visits America for the first time. He walks up and down the aisles of a grocery store with his son.

Dad: Vas diss? Powdered orange juice?
Son: Yeah, Dad. You just add a little water, and you have fresh orange juice.

A few minutes later, in a different aisle...
Dad: Und vas diss? Powdered milk?
Son: Yeah, Dad. You just add a little water, and you have fresh milk.

A few minutes later, in a different aisle...
Dad: Son, come give a look here! Baby powder! Vat a country, vat a country!

FISH CAKES WITH REMOULADE SAUCE

1/2 cup butter
1/2 cup onion, chopped
1/4 cup sweet red bell pepper, chopped
  1 lb cooked fish (such as cod, haddock, or whiting)
  1 cup bread crumbs
1/4 tsp Cajun seasoning (See page 182)
1/2 tsp Herbamare or other herbal seasoning blend
  1 tsp wheat-free tamari soy sauce
1/2 Tbsp Dijon mustard
  2 eggs, beaten
    Whole wheat flour to coat

Sauté onion and red bell pepper in 2 tablespoons butter.

Break cooked fish into small pieces and place in large bowl. Add onion, bell pepper, and all other ingredients except whole wheat flour and remaining butter; mix together. Form fish cakes and coat with flour.

Melt remaining butter in large frying pan. Cook fish cakes on medium heat for five minutes on each side, until golden brown. Serve with Remoulade Sauce.

Makes about 12 fish cakes

Remoulade Sauce

3/4 cup mayonnaise (See page 191)
1/4 cup Dijon mustard
  1 Tbsp honey
  2 tsp ketchup
1/2 tsp apple cider vinegar
1/2 tsp cayenne pepper
1/2 tsp paprika

Mix all ingredients. Chill before serving with fish cakes.

Makes 1 cup sauce

GRILLED SALMON WITH FAITH SAUCE

    4 6-oz wild-caught salmon filets
3/4 cup butter
    8 cloves garlic, minced
    1 tsp sea salt
    1 tsp fresh ground black pepper
1/2 cup packed fresh, snipped parsley

Melt butter in small saucepan. Add garlic, salt, pepper, and parsley; simmer for a few minutes. Brush both sides of salmon with 1/3 of the sauce and allow salmon to marinate for about an hour.

Grill salmon 4 to 5 minutes per side, depending on thickness of filets, basting with sauce frequently while cooking. (Grill salmon meat side down first and skin side down last. This will keep salmon from falling apart once it becomes tender. As the skin cooks it becomes crispy and the scales cook away, so the skin can be eaten too. The skin contains good oils our bodies need.)

Serve over brown rice with fresh vegetables or potatoes.

Extra Faith Sauce may be drizzled over salmon and rice, vegetables, and/or potatoes.

Serves 4

~ Salmon is also great broiled in the oven when grilling is unfeasible.

~ We refer to this sauce as Faith Sauce because it was our friend Faith Jones who introduced us to this simple yet delicious dish.

~ This dish is loaded with beneficial properties.
Salmon is a great source of healthy omega-3 essential fatty acids and contains several important vitamins. *Fresh parsley* contains glutathione, which serves as an antioxidant and even protects against cataracts.

GRILLED SALMON WITH FAITH SAUCE (Cont.)

Garlic is great for heart health and studies have also shown it to be a combatant to cancer, particularly colon, prostate, and stomach cancer. This recipe may be garlic overload for those not used to eating a lot of fresh garlic, as we are. Adjust the recipe accordingly but try to work your way up to increased garlic use.

$ Money Saving Tip $

Clip coupons.

We have saved 30, 50, even 80% of our grocery bill by using coupons. The savings really skyrocket when we use a coupon to purchase a product that is on sale.

Many health food stores offer free coupon books to their customers. If you like a certain brand, check out its website; usually they have downloadable coupons.

Think you don't have time to clip coupons? Clip them while at home chatting with family or friends, or while you are talking on the phone.

When you get to the cash register, you will realize that the money-saving benefits are well worth the time spent clipping coupons!

MEDITERRANEAN TUNA SALAD SANDWICHES

2 6-oz cans light tuna (packed in water), drained
1 6.5-oz jar marinated artichoke hearts, drained and chopped
1/4 cup chopped black olives
1/2 cup chopped red bell pepper
1/2 cup finely chopped red onion
1/3 cup mayonnaise (See page 191)
1 Tbsp lemon juice
2 tsp capers
Fresh ground pepper, to taste

In a large bowl, combine all ingredients. Serve on toasted whole grain bread.

Serves 4

~ Optional additions: Parsley, basil, garlic, oregano.

~ Some people enjoy tuna salad atop a green salad.

~ Buy artichoke hearts that are packed in oil, not water. They have more flavor.

~ This is not an average tuna salad. Even if capers or artichoke hearts don't appeal to you, go ahead and give this a try. You'll be surprised how good it is.

Biblical Broiled Fish

"And they gave him [Jesus] a piece of a broiled fish, and of an honeycomb.
And he took it, and did eat before them."

Luke 24:42-43

PECAN CRUSTED HALIBUT*

     8 6-oz halibut steaks
     1 cup whole grain flour
 1/2 tsp sea salt
 3/4 tsp ground pepper
     2 tsp coarse ground Dijon mustard
     2 large eggs
1-1/4 cups finely chopped pecans
1-1/4 cups bread crumbs
     2 Tbsp butter
     Prepared brown rice

In a shallow bowl, mix flour, salt, and pepper. In another shallow bowl, whisk together mustard and eggs. Place pecans and bread crumbs in third shallow bowl. Dredge fish in the flour mixture, then dip it in the egg mixture. Coat fish in pecan-bread crumb mixture.

Melt butter over medium heat. Cook steaks 2 to 3 minutes on each side or till lightly browned. Add butter as needed. Put steaks on foil covered baking sheet. Bake in preheated 350° oven for 10 to 12 minutes. While fish is baking, prepare Mustard Cream Sauce.

Place desired amount of brown rice on each plate, place halibut steak on top, and drizzle it with sauce.

Serves 8 (This recipe is easily halved or quartered if you are serving four or two people instead of eight.)

Mustard Cream Sauce

    1 cup heavy cream
1/2 cup coarse ground Dijon mustard
    Sea salt and pepper

In small saucepan, combine cream and mustard; whisk over low heat for three minutes. Add salt and pepper.

* Recipe Contributed by Bea Ferrin

SPICY FISH TACOS

1-1/4 lb tilapia filets
2 to 3 tsp organic taco seasoning
    8 taco shells or taco-sized corn or flour tortillas,
        warmed
    Sour cream
    Salsa
    Lettuce, chopped
    Avocado, sliced
    Shredded raw cheddar cheese

Sprinkle tilapia with taco seasoning.

In a lightly oiled skillet, cook tilapia for 2 to 4 minutes per side. When almost done, break up the fish with a spatula into 1 to 2 inch pieces.

Place all ingredients on table and serve buffet style.

Serves 4

Fish Fun

Whether you broil, grill or bake, "clean" fish is one of the healthiest and easiest foods you can prepare. Try haddock, tilapia, trout, salmon, sole, orange roughy, halibut, and flounder.
Season with organic spices of your choice.
Some fish is good lightly fried in a small amount of healthy oil, such as coconut.

Need tartar sauce for your fish? It's easy to prepare. Simply mix mayonnaise and sweet pickle relish together, to taste.

POULTRY

BEANS AND CHICKEN WRAPS*

2 15-1/2 oz cans organic black beans, drained
1 cup salsa
1 tsp ground cumin
1 tsp chili powder
1/2 tsp salt
1 whole chicken, cooked, deboned, and shredded
Grated sharp cheddar cheese, if desired

Combine all ingredients except chicken and cheddar cheese in saucepan. Simmer mixture over medium heat, uncovered, about 15 minutes; stir occasionally.

Roll beans and chicken into tortillas. Add cheese, if desired; wrap. This is a quick and easy but delicious and filling meal.

Serves 6 to 8

* Recipe Contributed by Bea Ferrin

Cast Iron Cooking

As people become more aware of the health dangers of using pots and pans made with carcinogenic materials, cast iron cookware is making a comeback.

Cast iron can be used to cook or bake. Food cooks evenly. If cast iron cookware is properly seasoned, food will not stick to it. For people low in iron, cooking with cast iron will increase dietary iron levels. Cast iron is not expensive but it is durable. If properly cared for, it will last a lifetime.

BUTTERMILK CHICKEN

        1 cup buttermilk
    3/4 cup onion, finely chopped
        1 Tbsp paprika
        1 tsp dried tarragon
1-1/2 tsp garlic powder
        1 tsp celery powder
    1/2 tsp freshly ground black pepper
        1 lb boneless skinless chicken thighs or breasts

Preheat oven to 350°.

In a bowl, combine all ingredients, except chicken, until well blended. Pour this mixture in a 9 x 13-inch baking pan. Add the chicken, coating it with the sauce.

Bake one hour, turning twice. Serve immediately.

Serves 6

Oil of Joy

"The Spirit of the Lord GOD is upon me; because the LORD hath anointed me to preach good tidings unto the meek; he hath sent me to bind up the brokenhearted, to proclaim liberty to the captives, and the opening of the prison to them that are bound; To proclaim the acceptable year of the LORD, and the day of vengeance of our God; to comfort all that mourn; To appoint unto them that mourn in Zion, to give unto them beauty for ashes, the *oil of joy* for mourning, the garment of praise for the spirit of heaviness; that they might be called trees of righteousness, the planting of the LORD, that he might be glorified."

Isaiah 61:1-3

CHICKEN AND CHEESE ENCHILADAS

1/4 cup oil
  1 clove garlic, minced
  1 medium yellow onion, minced
  2 cups tomato sauce
  1 tsp dried oregano
  1 tsp sea salt
1-1/2 cups shredded cooked chicken
  8 6-inch whole-wheat or spelt tortillas
  1 4-oz can chopped green chilies, drained
  2 cups grated sharp or extra sharp cheddar cheese
  1 cup sour cream
  Salsa

Preheat oven to 350°.

Combine 2 tablespoons of the oil, garlic, and onion in a 1-quart saucepan. Cook over low to medium heat until onions are translucent, about five minutes, stirring occasionally. Add tomato sauce, oregano, and salt. Simmer, uncovered, for 15 minutes.

Meanwhile, season chicken with *1/2 teaspoon garlic salt* and *1/2 teaspoon pepper*. Heat remaining oil in skillet; add chicken and cook.

Evenly distribute chicken and chilies among the tortillas. Sprinkle a little cheese over the chicken and chilies. Roll the tortillas up and place them in a 9 x 13-inch baking dish that has been lightly coated with oil. Cover with tomato sauce, and sprinkle with cheese.

Cover and bake for about 15 minutes, until the cheese is melted and bubbly. Serve with sour cream and salsa.

~ To make Beef and Cheese Enchiladas, follow all directions for Chicken and Cheese Enchiladas, except substitute 2 cups cooked ground beef for the chicken.

CHICKEN DIVAN

  3 cups seasoned and cooked chicken,
      chopped into bite-sized pieces
  4 cups fresh broccoli, chopped
  1/2 cup butter
  1/2 cup flour
  1/3 tsp black pepper
  1/8 tsp ground nutmeg
2-1/4 cups light cream or milk
  2 cups chicken broth
  1/2 medium onion, chopped
  2 cups grated Swiss cheese
  6 Tbsp grated Parmesan cheese
  Paprika
  Prepared brown rice

Lightly sauté or steam broccoli. Distribute evenly in the bottom of a 9 x 13-inch baking dish.

For sauce, melt butter in a 2-quart saucepan at low-medium heat. Stir in flour, pepper, and nutmeg to create a paste. Add cream or milk, chicken broth, and onion. Turn heat to medium. Cook and stir until thick and bubbly. Add Swiss cheese, stirring until cheese melts.

Pour half of the sauce over the broccoli. Top with chicken, then the remaining sauce. Sprinkle Parmesan cheese on top. Liberally sprinkle paprika on top as well.

Bake in a 350° oven for about 20 minutes.

Serve over desired amount of brown rice.

~ Turkey may be used instead of chicken.

CHICKEN LETTUCE WRAPS

2 Tbsp olive oil
2 cloves garlic, minced
1 small onion, diced
2 Tbsp ginger, minced
1 lb chicken, sliced into strips, then cooked
4 oz water chestnuts, sliced into strips
3 Tbsp soy sauce
2 Tbsp hoisin sauce
1 Tbsp honey
1/2 tsp white pepper
1 bunch green onions, diced
1 head bibb or butter (Boston) lettuce,
    leaves separated
Carrots, sliced into thin, long strips
Thai Peanut Sauce (See page 193)

Heat oil in a large sauté pan. Add garlic, onion, and ginger. Cook 5 minutes. Add chicken and water chestnuts. Cook 5 minutes, then add soy sauce, hoisin sauce, honey, and white pepper. Cook 5 more minutes, stirring occasionally. Add green onions.

Wrap in lettuce leaves and serve with carrots and Thai Peanut Sauce.

Serves 4

~ Pleasantly light but satisfyingly filling. These are so good, even junk food fans will like them.

Dredging

Dredging means to coat a food such as chicken or fish with a dry ingredient (such as flour, corn meal, or bread crumbs) before cooking or baking it.

CHICKEN SATAY

4 boneless, skinless chicken breasts
(about 1-1/2 lb)
3/4 cup coconut milk (not coconut cream)
1-1/2 Tbsp green curry paste
1 Tbsp soy sauce
16 12-inch wooden skewers

Place skewers in enough water to cover and let soak at least one-half hour.

Place chicken breasts between wax paper or in a one-gallon Ziploc bag and pound chicken to between 1/8- and 1/4-inch thick. (This makes meat tender and easier to thread onto skewers.) Cut chicken diagonally into 1-inch strips; set aside.

In medium bowl combine coconut milk, curry paste and soy sauce for marinade. Mix well. Add chicken to marinade a few pieces at a time, coating well. Let stand in bowl for 20 minutes.

Start charcoal fire or turn on gas grill for medium heat.

Thread chicken strips onto skewers accordion style and discard excess marinade. Place chicken skewers on hot grill and cook 3 to 4 minutes per side, covered. Serve with Thai Peanut Sauce (See page 193).

Serves 4

Briquets

It is best to avoid more common charcoal briquets that contain chemicals and fillers. The smoke they release can produce carcinogens in food. Use all-natural hardwood charcoal briquets instead.

CHICKEN STIR FRY

1 Tbsp oil
1 lb boneless, skinless chicken breasts, seasoned
1/2 red bell pepper
1/2 yellow bell pepper
1/2 orange bell pepper
1/2 green bell pepper
1/2 portabella mushroom
1 small onion
1 cup broccoli
1/4 cup wheat-free tamari soy sauce
2 Tbsp honey

In a medium bowl, blend soy sauce and honey. Cut all vegetables in strips. Marinate bell peppers and onions in soy sauce-honey mixture for 15 minutes. Stir frequently.

In large skillet or wok, heat oil and add chicken. Cook till done. Remove from pan and cut into strips; set aside.

In the same pan, sauté bell peppers and onions 3 minutes. Add broccoli and mushrooms; cook 2 minutes. Add chicken and soy sauce-honey marinade to pan and stir vegetables and chicken together; cook 2 minutes. Do not overcook vegetables; they should be tender-crisp.

Serve over brown rice, if desired.

Serves 6 to 8

Stir Frying

Stir frying means to cook foods quickly over high or medium-high heat, using a small amount of oil. A wok or skillet is normally used. The food must be stirred continually. Vegetables should not be browned, but cooked just till they are tender-crisp.

CURRY CHICKEN #1

4 Tbsp butter
1 Tbsp arrowroot powder or 3 Tbsp whole grain flour
2 Tbsp curry powder, more if desired
2 cups coconut milk
1 Tbsp chopped onion
2 cups diced cooked chicken
1 Tbsp honey
 Sea salt and pepper to taste
 Prepared brown rice
1/2 Tbsp lemon juice

In large saucepan, melt butter, then add arrowroot powder or flour and curry powder; stir to form paste. Pour in coconut milk and stir well, just until boiling. Add onion, chicken, honey, salt and pepper. Serve over desired amount of brown rice. Add lemon juice when ready to serve.

Serves 4

~ Bill's special addition: After adding onion, chicken, honey, salt and pepper, stir in 4 tablespoons natural peanut butter. Remove from heat immediately so the oil in the peanut butter does not separate.

~ Curry Chicken may be served over vegetables instead of or in addition to brown rice. Simply marinate bite sized pieces of bell pepper, onion, carrots, broccoli, and portabella mushrooms in 2 tablespoons olive oil and 1/2 tablespoon soy sauce for at least an hour. Sauté over medium-high heat and serve.

Simmering

Simmering is cooking food just below the boiling point. If food begins to boil, heat must be reduced.

CURRY CHICKEN #2*

3 Tbsp butter
1/4 cup chopped onion
3 tsp curry powder
3 Tbsp whole grain flour
1/4 tsp ginger
3/4 tsp sea salt
1 cup chicken broth
1 cup milk or coconut milk
1 tsp honey
2 cups cooked, shredded chicken,
   seasoned with salt, pepper, and garlic powder
1/2 tsp lemon juice
4 cups cooked brown rice

In large skillet, over low to medium heat, simmer onions in butter till translucent; stir in curry powder. Add flour, ginger, and sea salt; cook slowly. Gradually add chicken broth, milk, and honey; cook and continue stirring until slightly thickened. Add chicken and lemon juice. Simmer for a few minutes and serve over brown rice.

Suggested Toppings: Raisins, dried cherries, shredded, unsweetened coconut, tomatoes, diced boiled eggs, chutney, pineapple chunks, peanuts. (These toppings may be placed on the table for individual selection.)

Serves 4

* This curry chicken recipe is adapted from the original served by Louise Bonney, a splendid and gracious hostess. Its flavor is not as heavy as that of Curry Chicken #1, for the benefit of those who like a lighter chicken curry. It is delicious and easy to prepare.

JAMAICAN JERK CHICKEN

1-1/2 Tbsp pimento grains
1-1/2 Tbsp fresh thyme
3 Tbsp garlic powder
5 Tbsp Walkers Wood Jamaican Jerk Seasoning
2 tsp browning sauce
1 Tbsp molasses
2 Tbsp honey
1-1/2 Tbsp water
2/3 cup minced onion
18 to 20 all-natural chicken legs
2 lemons

Step One
To create marinade, combine first nine ingredients in a 1-quart bowl. Mix thoroughly and set aside.

Step Two
Remove skin from chicken and make three deep cuts into each piece lengthwise. Do not cut all the way to the bone. Space the cuts evenly around the leg. These cuts allow faster cooking and also help the flavor of the marinade to penetrate into the meat.

Step Three
Squeeze the juice from the lemons into a 2-quart bowl and dredge chicken pieces through the lemon juice. Place chicken on a clean plate and let stand for 10 minutes. Drain off excess lemon juice, then pat the chicken dry using paper towels.

Step Four
Take 3 or 4 pieces of chicken at a time and place in the jerk marinade, rubbing the marinade into the cuts. Do this until all chicken has been rubbed. Place the chicken and remaining marinade in a 1-gallon Ziploc bag; let sit in refrigerator for at least 6 hours or overnight, turning the bag over every few hours.

JAMAICAN JERK CHICKEN (Cont.)

Step Five
When ready to cook, remove chicken from marinade making sure pimento grains are removed and discarded. Place chicken on plate or platter. Set marinade aside for Jerk Sauce.

Step Six
Chicken may be cooked on a grill or in the oven.
~ Grill Method: Cook at low to medium heat for 45 minutes to 1 hour or until chicken is fully cooked. Turn frequently to prevent burning. Keep lid of grill closed unless turning.
~ Oven Method: Preheat oven to 350°. Cover bottom of pan in aluminum foil for easy clean up. Brush foil with light amount of butter or oil. Place chicken in pan and cover, cooking for 30 minutes. Remove cover and let brown, cooking for additional 45 minutes or until done. Turn chicken every 10 to 15 minutes.

Step Seven
Serve chicken with rice and Jerk Sauce.

~ Chicken thighs may be used instead of chicken legs.

~ Chicken is not as spicy the day after it's cooked.

Jerk Sauce

1 cup milk
1 cup water
3-1/2 tsp Better than Bouillon Chicken Base
2 tsp browning sauce
1 Tbsp jerk marinade (or more for spicier sauce)
4 Tbsp cold water and 2 Tbsp flour for thickener

JAMAICAN JERK CHICKEN (Cont.)

Place milk, water, Better than Bouillon, browning sauce and marinade in small saucepan. Bring to boil. Reduce heat and simmer for 5 minutes. Continue adding marinade until desired spiciness is reached.

To thicken sauce, put 2 tablespoons flour and 4 tablespoons cold water in a small jar. Put the lid on the jar and shake until flour is dissolved. Pour blended flour-water mixture into sauce and stir for a few minutes, as sauce simmers. Repeat this step a few times, if necessary, to achieve desired thickness.

Simmer till hot and serve with Jamaican Jerk Chicken.

What is Jamaican Jerk?

Jamaican Jerk is a cooking style in which meat is rubbed with a special spicy seasoning, marinated for 6 to 12 hours, and then cooked over an open fire. It is turned (jerked) over and over again to prevent burning.

Jerk Seasoning is a unique blend of spices which includes pimento, Scotch bonnet peppers, scallions, thyme, nutmeg, salt, and black pepper and sometimes garlic, cinnamon, and cloves.

Pimento is another name for allspice. Allspice is from a plant called "Pimenta dioica." Pimento grains look similar to peppercorns.

QUICK CHICKEN QUESADILLAS

2 cups shredded raw Cheddar or Monterey Jack
cheese
1 cup chicken, cooked and shredded
1/4 cup sliced green onions
6 whole wheat or spelt flour tortillas
Sour cream
Salsa

Preheat oven to 350°. Lightly oil a large baking sheet.

Spread 1/3 cup cheese evenly over half of each tortilla. Evenly distribute chicken and green onions over cheese. Fold tortillas in half.

Bake 5 to 6 minutes or till cheese is melted.

Cut folded tortillas into quarters; serve with sour cream and salsa.

Makes 6 quesadillas

~ How easy can you get? These are great reheated for quick lunches.

Cheddar Cheese

We prefer extra sharp cheddar cheese to mild cheddar cheese. The sharpness of cheese is determined by how long it has been aged. Mild cheddars have usually been aged for 2 to 3 months; extra sharp cheddars are aged for a year or longer.

If you buy cheddar in a block, chill it in the refrigerator for about 30 minutes before grating it. It will grate better than if it is warm.

SIMPLE SAUCE FOR CHICKEN

1 cup coconut oil
1/2 cup balsamic vinegar
2 tsp honey
2 tsp honey mustard (See page 182)
2 tsp soy sauce

Put all ingredients in a small pan. Cook at medium heat until fully blended and somewhat thick.

Use this sauce for oven baked or grilled chicken legs and thighs. Baste chicken with the sauce when the chicken is almost done.

Terra Cotta Cooking

The literal translation for "terra cotta" is "baked earth." Terra cotta cookware is clay-based and has been used since ancient times.

We were delighted the first time we roasted a chicken in a terra cotta pan. The chicken was a beautiful golden color, crispy on the outside and tender on the inside. Terra cotta holds in moisture so food is juicy and evenly cooked.

Some people use terra cotta to cook most anything from soups and stews to beef, vegetables and roasted garlic.

Terra cotta can be expensive but it is well worth the investment. The flavors are unbeatable.

TURKEY AND SMOKED GOUDA SANDWICH

1 serving ciabatta bread
1 ounce (approximately) smoked Gouda cheese,
    thinly sliced with rind removed
3 to 4 slices turkey breast
    Tomato slices
    Thinly sliced onion

Slice bread. On the bottom piece of bread, layer Gouda cheese, turkey breast, tomato slices, and onion slices. Place top piece of bread over onion.

Lightly wrap sandwich in aluminum foil and place on a cookie sheet. Bake at 325° for 15 minutes.

Serve immediately.

Makes 1 sandwich

~ Ciabatta bread is a rustic bread with a heavy crust. French or Italian bread may be substituted if necessary.

~ This sandwich is quick and easy to prepare and is delicious and filling. Smoked Gouda is a tasty Dutch cheese that becomes creamy when melted.

Better than Bouillon

Organic Better than Bouillon Food Bases are good alternatives to conventional (and very unhealthy) bouillon cubes. Available in beef, chicken, turkey, mushroom, and vegetable, these bases are good to have on hand when you need stock or broth.

TURKEY BURGERS
WITH SUNDRIED TOMATOES

1/4 lb white ground turkey
1/4 lb dark ground turkey
1/8 tsp pepper
1/8 tsp cumin
1/4 tsp salt
  1 tsp dried parsley
1/2 cup whole wheat bread crumbs
1/2 tsp garlic powder or 1 clove garlic, minced
1/2 Tbsp balsamic vinegar
1/8 cup minced onion
  3 sundried tomatoes in olive oil, chopped
     plus 1 Tbsp olive oil from the jar
  1 egg white
  Caramelized Onions (See page 183)
  3 whole wheat burger buns, toasted

With your hands, gently mix together all ingredients, except caramelized onions, in a large bowl. Take care to not overwork the mixture.

Form into three patties, making an indentation in the middle of each one to help the burgers cook evenly. Cover and refrigerate 30 to 60 minutes to blend flavors.

Place patties in lightly oiled skillet over medium-high heat. Cook 3 to 5 minutes per side, or till all pink is gone from center and burgers are browned. If using cheese, place it on patties after turning the burgers. Top with caramelized onions. Place burgers on buns and serve with sides such as lettuce, tomato slices, and condiments.

Serves 3

~ Ground turkey is a nice alternative to ground beef. These are also great grilled.

Pizza with Pizzazz

Use the ideas below to top your pizzas. Be creative; you might create award winning pizzas!

Fresh herbs like basil, oregano, or chives

~

Fresh vegetables such as bell peppers, broccoli, zucchini, eggplant, mushrooms, spinach, or tomatoes

~

Caramelized onions or bell peppers

~

Roasted garlic cloves

~

Red onions, shallots, or scallions

~

Sliced black or Kalamata olives

~

Pineapple chunks

~

Sundried tomatoes

~

Anchovies

~

Crushed red pepper

~

Mozzarella, chèvre, feta, asiago, or Parmesan cheese

~

Seasoned, cooked, sliced chicken

~

Uncured pepperoni slices

Use pesto for an occasional change from traditional tomato sauce. Also, instead of refined white flour crusts, use whole grain crusts.

See page 192 to make homemade Pizza Sauce.

BEEF
AND
LAMB

GREEK STYLE LAMB CHOPS

1 8-bone rack of lamb
1-1/2 cups olive oil
    2 Tbsp crushed dried oregano
    2 lemons
    1 Tbsp butter
    1 large onion, sliced into 1/8-inch strips
    6 cloves garlic minced
1/4 tsp salt or to taste
1/2 tsp pepper

Step One
When purchasing the rack of lamb, ask the butcher to make sure the thin skin on the outside of the rack is removed and ask him to cut off the chine bone to make rack easier to carve.

Step Two
Divide lamb into 8 individual chops. Place chops in a one-gallon Ziploc bag with juice of one lemon, 2 cloves garlic, onions, oregano, salt, pepper and olive oil. Remove air from bag and mix very well. Let stand at room temperature for one hour before placing into the refrigerator.

Step Three
Take out and mix ingredients every hour or so if possible. If oil begins to thicken, allow it to warm up for a little while so flavors can meld. Let ingredients marinate for at least 6 hours or overnight.

Step Four
When ready to cook, remove lamb and onions from oil; reserve the oil. Separate lamb and onions and place on two different plates to allow some of the excess oil to drain off the lamb. There will still be enough oil on them to cook.

GREEK STYLE LAMB CHOPS (Cont.)

Step Five
Place two teaspoons of the marinade oil and 2 cloves of garlic in a large skillet or frying pan. Simmer for two minutes. Add onions, a little pepper and continue to simmer, covered, about twenty minutes, stirring occasionally. Squeeze 1/2 of second lemon into onions, mixing lemon juice into onions. Turn heat to medium-high and cook, uncovered, for 6 more minutes allowing onions to brown a little while scraping the bottom of pan every few minutes. Remove from heat and set onions aside in small bowl.

Step Six
Lamb may be fried or grilled.
~ Frying Method: In same pan or skillet place two teaspoons of marinade oil and two remaining cloves of garlic. Simmer for two minutes. Add 1 tablespoon real butter and lamb chops. Cook on medium-high heat about 4 to 6 minutes per side, or until desired doneness is reached.
~ Grilling Method: Cook on high heat. Put a little oil on grill to keep from sticking. Place lamb chops on hot grill rack with tongs, not fork. Cook 4 to 5 minutes per side depending on thickness of chops and desired doneness of meat.

Step Seven
Place four chops on a plate with onions and wedge of lemon.

Serves 2

~ These lamb chops are great served with steamed vegetables and garlic mashed potatoes.

MEAT LOAF

1/8 tsp each dried sage, basil, dill, oregano, thyme,
     garlic powder, and onion powder
1/4 tsp salt
1/4 tsp pepper
  2 Tbsp fresh parsley, snipped
1/8 cup whole wheat flour
1/2 cup whole oats
1/4 cup milk, water, or apple juice
1/2 cup onion, chopped fine
  1 egg
  1 lb ground beef

In a mixing bowl combine all ingredients except ground
beef. When mixed, add ground beef and mix again.
Press into an 8 x 11-inch loaf pan. Bake at 350° for 45
minutes. Remove from oven and apply topping. Bake
15 to 20 minutes more.

Meat Loaf Topping

  1 tsp mustard
1/4 cup honey
1/2 cup ketchup

Mix together and apply to top of meatloaf.

Terrific TLTs

TLTs are BLTs with turkey "bacon" instead of pork
bacon. Choose turkey bacon that is antibiotic free,
organic if possible. Add organic lettuce and fresh
tomato slices. Use your own homemade
mayonnaise (See page 191). These make for a
filling, delicious breakfast or lunch.

SHEPHERDS PIE

1 cup onion, chopped
2 lb ground beef, seasoned
3 cups corn
    (Corn shucked fresh from the cob is the best.)
4 cups mashed potatoes (about 12 medium potatoes)
1 cup sharp or extra sharp cheddar cheese, grated

In large pan, brown ground beef. Drain fat if necessary and transfer meat to 9 x 13-inch baking dish; add preferred seasonings.

In the same large pan, sauté onions. Mix together with meat. Spread evenly. Layer corn, potatoes, and cheese over meat-onion mixture.

Cook at 375° till cheese is melted and potatoes are golden.

~ This traditional dish is quick and easy and sure to satisfy hearty appetites. You can also try adding carrots, green beans, and peas, along with the spices thyme, marjoram, and fresh basil. Feel free to experiment with proportions. In addition to the corn, you might want to use mixed vegetables.

Preserving Purity

"What we need in this country is a general improvement in eating. We have the best raw materials in the world, both quantitatively and qualitatively, but most of them are ruined in the process of preparing them for the table."

H.L. Mencken

$ Money Saving Tip $

"Eating healthy is so expensive!"

When we talk to people about eating healthy,
the first thing we usually hear is,
"It costs so much to eat like that!"
With this statement, people convince themselves
that they are unable to purchase healthy food.
Yet many people that say this think nothing of
spending money to support costly hobbies,
recreational activities, pets, etc., etc., etc.
For most people, eating better is not a matter of
expense; it's a matter of priorities.

I remember how years ago we stood at a
crossroads. It did seem expensive to eat healthy.
As evangelists, our income is modest and
unpredictable. But we believed it was wise to
change some of our habits so we began stocking
our kitchen with staples and organic groceries
from health food stores. We considered our
purchases long term investments.

Instead of paying top dollar for every product all
the time, we learned ways to save money.
We live simply. We don't eat out a lot. We don't
have expensive hobbies. We keep our debts low
or nonexistent. We consider good stewardship of
our bodies a priority. Through the years, God
has honored our desire to take care of our
bodies and has provided for us. We have
discovered that eating healthy is not as
expensive as it seemed years ago.

COOKIES AND BARS

BLUEBERRY COOKIES

2 cups whole wheat flour
1/2 tsp sea salt
1/2 tsp cinnamon
2 tsp baking powder (See page 143)
1 cup fresh blueberries
1/2 cup organic all-vegetable shortening
1/2 cup honey
1-1/2 tsp grated lemon peel
1 egg
1/4 cup milk

Combine flour, salt, cinnamon, and baking powder in a small bowl. Stir in blueberries. Set aside.

In a larger bowl, combine shortening and honey, then add lemon peel and egg; beat until smooth. Alternately add flour mixture and milk, stirring thoroughly after each addition.

Drop by teaspoonfuls onto oiled cookie sheet. Bake at 375° for about 10 minutes, or until lightly browned.

Makes 3 dozen

Poetic Moment

It doesn't matter what the time of year,
Homemade cookies are sure to appear.

Keeping them healthy, preservative free,
Oats, whole wheat flour, a little honey.

CAROB MOLASSES COOKIES

3 cups whole wheat flour
1/2 cup carob powder
1 tsp baking soda
3/4 cup unsweetened organic applesauce
3/4 cup unsulphured organic molasses
2 tsp vanilla
1/2 cup chopped walnuts

Mix together flour, carob powder, and baking soda. Stir in applesauce, molasses and vanilla; blend well. Stir in walnuts.

Chill in refrigerator at least 30 minutes. Roll into balls and place on oiled baking sheet. Bake at 350° for about 10 minutes.

Makes about 3-1/2 dozen

~ They are incredibly easy to make. If you are not used to carob, you might want to use 1/4 cup carob powder and 1/4 cup cocoa powder in place of 1/2 cup carob powder.

~ There are several varieties of molasses: light and very sweet, dark and moderately sweet, and blackstrap, which is very dark and kind of bitter. Be sure to always buy unsulphured molasses.

Carob for Generations

"As my forefathers planted carob trees for me, so I shall plant for my children."

Babylonian Talmud

CASHEW-PEANUT BARS

1 tsp salt
1/2 cup peanuts
1/2 cup sunflower seeds
1/2 cup pumpkin seeds
1 cup dried, unsulphured mango, papaya,
   pineapple, cranberries, raisins
   (or a combination), cut into small pieces
1 cup oats
2-1/2 cups raw cashews
1/2 cup honey, divided

Mix together all ingredients except the honey. Stir in 1/4 cup honey. Spread evenly in an oiled 9 x 13-inch pan; pat together with spatula. Drizzle remaining 1/4 cup honey on top. Bake at 350° for about 20 minutes.

When cool, cut into bars.

I Cup White Sugar Equivalents

Raw Honey	1/2 to 3/4 cup
Maple Syrup	1/2 to 3/4 cup
Molasses	1/2 to 3/4 cup
Blackstrap Molasses	3/4 to 1 cup
Sorghum	1-1/3 cups
Brown Rice Syrup	1 to 1-1/2 cups
Barley Malt Syrup	1 to 1-1/2 cups
Fresh Fruit Juice Concentrate	1 cup
Frozen Fruit Juice Concentrate	1/2 cup
Rapadura	1 cup
Date Sugar	2/3 to 1 cup
Maple Sugar	1/2 cup
Turbinado Sugar	1 cup
Stevia	1 tsp to 2 Tbsp
Xylitol	1 cup

CLOUD COOKIES

1/2 cup butter, softened
3/4 cup honey
1/4 cup brown rice syrup
   2 large or 3 medium eggs
   2 tsp vanilla
   2 tsp freshly squeezed lemon juice
   1 cup thick sour cream
   2 tsp baking soda
3-1/2 cups wheat flour
   2 tsp baking powder (See page 143)
   1/2 tsp salt
   2 tsp cinnamon

In a large bowl, combine butter, honey, and brown rice syrup. Add eggs, vanilla, lemon juice, and sour cream; beat until smooth.

Add dry ingredients and stir until stiff batter is formed.

Drop by teaspoons onto a greased cookie sheet. Bake about 10 minutes at 350°.

Makes 5 dozen

~ This is a slightly sweet, refreshingly different cookie.

~ If desired, 1 cup pecans may be added to the batter.

The Best Cookies

"I am still convinced that a good, simple, homemade cookie is preferable to all the store-bought cookies one can find."

James Beard

CRANBERRY OAT COOKIES

1-1/2 cups whole wheat flour
1-1/2 cups rolled oats
  1/2 tsp baking soda
  1/2 tsp baking powder (See page 143)
  1/2 tsp salt
  1/2 tsp nutmeg
    2 tsp cinnamon
  1/4 cup oil
  1/4 cup unsweetened applesauce
  1/2 cup honey
    1 Tbsp molasses
    1 egg, beaten with 1 Tbsp water
    1 tsp vanilla
  3/4 cup dried cranberries
  1/2 cup chopped walnuts

In large bowl, mix together flour, oats, baking soda, baking powder, salt, nutmeg, and cinnamon. In medium bowl, mix together oil, applesauce, honey, molasses, egg, and vanilla. Mix wet ingredients into dry ingredients. Mix in cranberries and walnuts.

Chill dough in refrigerator for 30 minutes.

Preheat oven to 325°. Drop by teaspoonfuls onto oiled baking sheet. Bake about 15 minutes, until cookies are golden on the bottom.

Makes 2-1/2 dozen

~ This is a scrumptious, not-too-sweet cookie, with a nice texture.

~ Look in the health food store for dried cranberries sweetened with fruit, such as apple juice. (Most dried cranberries are sweetened with white sugar.)

GINGER COOKIES

1/2 cup softened butter
1/4 cup honey
3/4 cup molasses
1 beaten egg
1/2 tsp vanilla
1 tsp baking powder (See below)
2 cups whole wheat flour
1-1/2 tsp baking soda
1/2 tsp cinnamon
1/2 tsp salt
2 tsp ginger

Cream butter, honey and molasses. Add egg, vanilla, and sifted dry ingredients. Chill until the dough is very cold. It can be set on ice. Roll into small balls and bake at 350° for 10 to 15 minutes.

Makes about 4 dozen

Homemade Baking Powder

1/2 cup arrowroot powder
1/2 cup cream of tartar
1/4 cup baking soda

Sift together several times.
Store in airtight container.

Making your own baking powder is easy and ensures that you avoid the aluminum in commercial baking powders. You may need to use a little more homemade baking powder in recipes than you would commercial baking powder.

GRANOLA BARS

2/3 cup butter
1/3 cup honey
1/3 cup molasses
 1 tsp vanilla
3-1/2 cups quick rolled oats
 1/2 cup unsulphured, unsweetened fine coconut
 3/4 cup chopped walnuts, pecans, and/or cashews
 1/2 cup almonds, sliced
 1/4 cup raw pumpkin seeds
 1/4 cup raw sunflower seeds
 1/8 cup flax seeds, ground
 1/4 cup sesame seeds, ground
 1/2 cup dried cranberries
 5 Tbsp organic cocoa powder, optional
 1/2 tsp cinnamon
 1/2 tsp salt
 1 egg

Melt butter; remove from heat and stir in honey, molasses, and vanilla. Set aside.

Mix all dry ingredients. Add the egg to the dry ingredients; then add the butter mixture, mixing well with a fork or whisk.

Press into a greased 9 x 13-inch pan. Bake at 350° for about 20 minutes. Cool completely before cutting into bars and removing from pan.

~ Try this recipe, then experiment and create your own granola bar recipe using your favorite healthy ingredients. Here are some ideas: Raisins, chopped, dried, unsulphured fruit (like apricots, cherries, or figs), peanuts, almond butter or natural, fresh ground peanut butter.

OATMEAL CHOCOLATE CHIP COOKIES

1-1/2 cups whole wheat flour
  1/2 cup grated unsweetened coconut, optional
  1/2 tsp cinnamon
    1 tsp sea salt
    2 tsp baking soda
    1 cup organic all-vegetable shortening
  3/4 cup honey
    1 tsp vanilla
    2 large eggs
    2 cups rolled oats
  12 oz semi-sweet grain sweetened chocolate chips
  3/4 cup pecans, optional

Preheat oven to 325°. Oil cookie sheets. Combine flour, coconut, cinnamon, salt, and baking soda. Beat together shortening, honey, and vanilla until creamy. Add eggs, beating until light and fluffy. Gradually beat in flour mixture and rolled oats. Stir in chocolate chips and pecans, if desired.

Drop batter by well-rounded teaspoonfuls onto cookie sheet. Bake 8 to 12 minutes, or until light golden brown. Remove from oven and wait two minutes before transferring to wire rack for complete cooling.

Makes 4-1/2 dozen

~ This is America's favorite cookie made a little healthier. If you like sweeter cookies, try using 1/3 cup molasses and 2/3 cup honey instead of just honey. (If you do this, decrease the amount of chocolate chips.)

OATMEAL COCONUT COOKIES

3/4 cup butter
1/2 cup brown rice syrup
1/4 cup honey
1/8 cup blackstrap molasses
   1 tsp vanilla
   1 tsp baking soda
   1 cup whole wheat flour
   3 cups oats
   1 cup finely grated unsweetened coconut

Cream together butter, sweeteners, and vanilla. Sift in the baking soda and flour. Add oats and coconut and mix well. Drop by teaspoonfuls on cookie sheet. Bake at 350° for 8 minutes.

Makes 4 dozen

~ If desired, add 1/2 cup carob chips and 1/2 cup grain sweetened chocolate chips.

Milk, Butter, and Honey

"And it shall come to pass in that day, that a man
shall nourish a young cow, and two sheep;
And it shall come to pass, for the abundance of
milk that they shall give he shall eat butter:
for butter and honey shall every one eat that is left
in the land."

Isaiah 7:21-22

PIES
AND
CAKES

APPLE PIE

2 9-inch pie crusts (See page 158)
6 cups apples, peeled, cored, and thinly sliced
3/4 cup Rapadura
1 Tbsp flour
1 tsp cinnamon
1/2 tsp nutmeg

Arrange bottom pie crust in pie plate.

In a bowl, combine Rapadura, flour, cinnamon, and nutmeg. Add apples and stir until apples are coated.

Evenly fill the bottom pie crust with this mixture, then arrange the top pie crust over it. Seal the edges and cut slits in the top. Cover the edge with a pie shield. Bake in a preheated 375° oven for 50 minutes. Remove the pie shield after about 30 minutes to crisp the edge.

Serves 6 to 8

~ Other sweeteners may be used in place of Rapadura. If using honey, arrange all other ingredients in the bottom pie crust and drizzle 1/2 to 3/4 cup honey over the top of the apple mixture before arranging top pie crust.

Brown Sugar

To make 1 cup brown sugar, use a fork to combine 1 cup evaporated cane juice with molasses. (Use 1 tablespoon molasses to make light brown sugar and 2 tablespoons to make dark brown sugar.)

Rapadura, sucanat, and turbinado can all be substituted 1:1 for brown sugar.

BLUEBERRY CAKE

2 cups whole wheat flour
3/4 tsp salt
2 tsp cinnamon
2-1/2 tsp baking powder (See page 143)
2/3 cup oil
3/4 cup honey
1 cup milk
2 tsp vanilla
3 eggs
1 cup walnuts
3 cups blueberries

Sift together flour, salt, cinnamon, and baking powder; set aside.

In a separate bowl, combine oil, honey, milk, and vanilla. Add eggs one at a time and beat until well blended.

Add flour mixture a little at a time and whisk to blend. Fold in nuts and blueberries.

Pour into a greased 9 x 13-inch baking dish.

Bake at 350° for about 45 minutes.

~ This cake is quick and easy. It is one of Bill's favorites.

Measuring Honey

Before measuring honey, lightly oil the measuring utensils and then run hot water over them.
This will help honey freely flow from the utensils.

CARROT CAKE

1/4 tsp ginger
1 tsp salt
1 tsp nutmeg
1 tsp allspice
3 tsp cinnamon
2 tsp baking powder (See page 143)
3 tsp baking soda
2-1/4 cups whole wheat flour
3 cups grated carrots
3/4 cups raisins, optional
1 cup ground nuts, optional
1-1/3 cups oil
1 cup honey
5 eggs, separated
Cream cheese frosting (See page184)

Preheat oven to 350°.

Sift dry ingredients together. Set aside.

Mix grated carrots, raisins, and nuts. Combine oil and honey and add to carrot mixture. Add carrot mixture to dry ingredients.

Separate eggs and beat yolks until frothy. Mix yolks into cake mixture. Beat egg whites until very stiff. Fold carefully into cake mixture.

Pour into lightly oiled tube pan or two lightly oiled loaf pans. Bake 45 minutes to an hour, or until inserted toothpick comes out dry.

Cool before cutting lengthwise to make layers. Apply frosting to center, top, and sides.

~ Recipe may be halved.

FIG CAKE

       1 cup butter
   1/2 cup honey
       5 eggs, separated
       3 cups figs or fig preserves, chopped
       3 cups whole wheat flour
       1 cup plain yogurt
       1 tsp salt
   1-1/2 Tbsp cinnamon
   1/4 cup raisins
       1 cup walnuts

In a large mixing bowl, cream butter and honey together; set aside.

With electric mixer, beat egg yolks until thick, about five minutes; add to butter-honey mixture.

Add figs; stir until smooth. Add flour and yogurt, alternating. Add salt, cinnamon, raisins and nuts.

With electric mixer, beat egg whites until soft peaks form, then fold into cake mixture.

Pour into greased 9 x 13-inch pan and bake at 350° for 90 minutes.

~ If using sweetened fig preserves, reduce honey to 1/4 cup.

The First Vitamins

"Adam and Eve ate the first vitamins, including the packages."

E.R. Squibb

HONEY APPLESAUCE CAKE

      3 cups whole wheat flour
1-1/2 tsp baking soda
   1/4 tsp sea salt
1-1/2 tsp cinnamon
   1/2 tsp nutmeg
   1/2 tsp cloves
   1/2 tsp ginger
      1 Tbsp ground flax seeds
   1/2 cup oil
      1 cup raw honey
      1 tsp vanilla
      2 eggs
1-1/2 cups unsweetened applesauce
      1 cup chopped nuts, optional

In medium bowl, mix together dry ingredients; set aside.

In a large bowl, stir together oil, honey, and vanilla until well blended.   Add eggs and mix well.   Add dry ingredients alternately with the applesauce, stirring until smooth. Add nuts, if desired.

Spread into an oiled 9 x 13-inch pan and bake in a preheated 325° oven for 20 minutes.

~ Cinnamon is delightfully aromatic and healthy. Try adding a teaspoon to your favorite cookies and cakes.

Perplexing Paradox

"We are living in a world today where lemonade is made from artificial flavors and furniture polish is made from real lemons."

Alfred E. Newman

KAMUT-WHOLE WHEAT PIE CRUST

1/2 cup kamut flour
1/2 cup whole wheat flour
1/4 tsp sea salt
1/3 cup organic, all vegetable, non-hydrogenated
      shortening
3 to 4 Tbsp ice cold water

In mixing bowl, stir together flour and salt. With pastry blender, cut in shortening until crumbly. Sprinkle water, 1 tablespoon at a time, over dough, gently mixing with a fork. Form dough into a ball. Roll out on floured surface and carefully transfer to pie plate. Trim edge and flute.

Makes 1 9 or 10-inch pie crust.

~ If you do not have kamut flour, 1 cup whole wheat flour may be used.

Eggcellent Tips

For fluffier eggs, allow eggs to sit at room temperature for about an hour before baking.

If you only need half an egg, lightly beat one egg, and then extract 1-1/2 tablespoons from the beaten egg.

If a recipe is not specific, use large eggs.

KEY LIME PIE

Homemade sweetened condensed milk (See page 28)
4 egg yolks
1/2 cup fresh squeezed key lime juice
1 9-inch graham cracker pie crust

Preheat oven to 350°.

In mixing bowl on low speed, blend sweetened condensed milk and egg yolks. Add key lime juice and mix well. Pour ingredients into pie crust.

Bake 15 minutes. Leave at room temperature until pie is no longer warm. Chill in refrigerator.

Serves 6 to 8

~ If desired, spread whipped cream (See page 194) on top of pie after it has chilled. Garnish with fresh raspberries.

Mock Graham Cracker Pie Crust

1 cup whole wheat flour
1/3 cup oil or 1 stick butter, melted
1/2 cup finely chopped nuts

In a pie pan, mix together flour, oil or butter, and nuts. Press firmly into round 9-inch pie pan.

Bake at 350° for 12 to 15 minutes.

Allow to cool before pouring in filling.

PUMPKIN-SWEET POTATO PIE

3/4 cup cooked pumpkin
3/4 cup cooked sweet potato
1/2 cup honey
   3 eggs, separated
   2 Tbsp arrowroot powder
1/4 tsp nutmeg
1/4 tsp ginger
1/4 tsp cloves
1/2 tsp salt
   1 tsp cinnamon
1-1/4 cups milk
   1 unbaked 9-inch pie crust (See page 158)

Combine all ingredients except the egg whites. Beat egg whites until stiff and fold into pumpkin mixture. Pour mixture into pie crust and cover edge with pie crust shield. Bake at 375° for about one hour.

Piles of Smiles

Question:
What do you get if you divide the circumference of a pumpkin by its diameter?

Answer:
Pumpkin pi.

Author Unknown

STRAWBERRY RHUBARB PIE

2 10-inch whole wheat pie crusts (See page 158)
3 cups fresh rhubarb, sliced into 3/4-inch pieces
1 cup honey
6 Tbsp arrowroot powder
1 tsp vanilla
3 cups thickly sliced fresh strawberries
1/4 tsp salt
1/4 tsp nutmeg
1/2 tsp cinnamon
2 Tbsp whole wheat flour

Roll out one crust and fit into a 10-inch pie plate; refrigerate. Refrigerate dough for the top crust also.

Put sliced rhubarb into a colander with a bowl underneath. Pour honey over rhubarb; drain 1 hour.

In saucepan, mix half of the drained honey with arrowroot powder. Heat until thickened over low heat, then add the rest of the honey. Remove from heat and stir in vanilla.

Preheat oven to 350°.

Mix rhubarb and strawberries together in bowl. Add honey mixture. In small bowl mix together salt, nutmeg, cinnamon and flour. Add to fruit and gently toss to mix.

Evenly spoon filling into prepared pie crust. Roll out top crust and place on top. Join crusts, fluting edges. Cut slits to vent steam.

Bake one hour.

Allow to cool, then refrigerate a few hours to set.

WHOLE WHEAT CHOCOLATE CAKE

        3 cups whole wheat flour
    2/3 cup cocoa powder
        1 Tbsp baking powder (See page 143)
1-1/2 tsp baking soda
    1/2 tsp sea salt
1-1/2 cups raw honey
1-1/4 cups mayonnaise (See page 191)
1-1/4 cups water
        1 Tbsp vanilla

Combine the dry ingredients and set aside. Combine the wet ingredients, using a whisk to fully blend. Gradually add the dry ingredients to the wet ingredients and mix until smooth.

Pour into a lightly greased 9 x 13-inch pan. Bake at 350° for about 30 minutes, or until an inserted toothpick comes out clean.

If desired, cake may be frosted with cream cheese frosting (See page 184).

~ Do not over bake or you will have one dry cake. (We speak from experience!)

~ After you try this healthy variation of chocolate cake, you just might decide to never again use a boxed chocolate cake mix!

Honey is Good

"My son, eat thou honey, because it is good; and the honeycomb, which is sweet to thy taste:"

Proverbs 24:13

WHOLE WHEAT PIE CRUST

1-1/4 cups whole wheat flour
  1/4 tsp salt
    4 Tbsp cold butter, cut into chunks
5 to 6 Tbsp ice cold water

In medium bowl, combine flour and salt. Cut in butter with pastry blender until mixture resembles coarse crumbs.

Mix in water, 1 tablespoon at a time, stirring lightly with fork after each addition until smooth dough is formed.

Pat dough into smooth round disk. Wrap and refrigerate until ready to use. Then, on floured surface, roll out dough with rolling pin to size of pie pan. Gently transfer crust to pie pan.

Makes 1 9 or 10-inch pie crust

~ This pie crust recipe is simple, easy and quick. It is the easiest pie crust recipe in this cookbook. So if you are a beginner at making pie crusts, start with this one.

Substitutions

Use 1 tablespoon arrowroot powder in place of
1 tablespoon corn starch or 2 tablespoons flour.

Use 1 cup plain yogurt in place of
1 cup sour cream.

If a recipe calls for 1 cup oil,
you can replace half of the oil with applesauce.

WILD BLUEBERRY PIE*

Filling:
8 cups fresh wild blueberries
1 cup turbinado (raw) sugar
1 tsp cinnamon
1 Tbsp lemon juice
4 Tbsp (rounded) corn starch

Measure all filling ingredients into saucepan. Cook over medium heat until thickness of pudding, stirring gently and often. Set aside.

Pastry:
2-2/3 cups white wheat flour
1 tsp salt
2 to 3 Tbsp turbinado sugar
1 cup shortening or butter
6 Tbsp cold water

In a medium bowl, combine flour, salt, and sugar.

Cut shortening or butter into dry ingredients with pastry blender. When fine and crumbly, add water. Use a fork to blend together. (Do *not* use your hands.)

Divide dough into two halves. Roll out first half to fit pie plate. Transfer dough to pie plate and add filling. Roll out second half of dough and place on top of pie; seal edge with fingers.

Bake at 400° for 30 to 35 minutes. Serve warm.

Makes 1 9-inch pie

~ Frozen blueberries may be used in place of fresh. Be sure to use all the liquid from the frozen blueberries. Also, instead of wild blueberries, you may use cultivated blueberries, which are larger and more common.

WILD BLUEBERRY PIE (Cont.)

* This recipe was contributed by Melanie Chandler. It is her original creation, which she has perfected through the years. It is an award winning pie! Twice it was deemed the "Best Double Crust Blueberry Pie" at the Annual Machias, Maine Wild Blueberry Festival. Melanie was also awarded for "Best Over-all Entry in Presentation." I encourage you to try this one; it is a treat for the taste buds.

Pie Crust Tips

For tender dough, handle it as little as possible.

Chill dough a few minutes to make rolling faster and easier.

To prevent a soggy crust, refrigerate it about 15 minutes before filling it.

If a recipe calls for a baked pie crust, prick bottom and sides of the crust with a fork. Bake at 450° for 10 to 12 minutes.

If a recipe calls for an unbaked pie crust, do not prick bottom and sides, unless directed to do so by your pie recipe.

It saves time to make extra pie crusts and freeze them for future use. Duplicate recipe as many times as desired, using separate bowls for each pie crust. Instead of rolling dough into pie crusts, shape dough into balls. Wrap and freeze.

DESSERTS

CREAM CHEESE PASTRIES

1/2 cup butter, softened
　1 cup cream cheese, softened
　2 cups whole wheat flour
1/2 cup raw honey
　1 Tbsp vanilla
　1 tsp salt
1/3 cup melted butter
　1 Tbsp cinnamon

Place 1/2 cup butter, cream cheese, and flour in a large bowl and use an electric mixer to combine. Form into a ball and leave in bowl in refrigerator for 12 to 24 hours.

Bring dough to room temperature. Stir in honey, vanilla, and salt. Add enough additional flour to retain elasticity of dough.

Roll dough onto floured surface to form a 13 x 16-inch rectangle. Cut dough widthwise to form three separate sections.

Combine 1/3 cup melted butter and cinnamon and brush each section with the mixture.

Roll each section lengthwise. Making gentle cuts, create eight separate pastries out of each section.

Place pastries on oiled baking sheet about 1 inch apart. Bake at 300° for about 30 minutes, or till done.

Store in refrigerator or freezer and reheat before serving, if desired.

Makes 24 pastries

~ These pastries are of Jewish origin. They are usually called "rugelach."

STRAWBERRY SHORTCAKE

2 cups whole wheat flour
3 tsp baking powder (See page 143)
1/2 tsp salt
3/4 cup milk
1/4 cup butter, melted
2 Tbsp honey or maple syrup
8 cups strawberries, sliced (about 4 pounds)
1/2 cup honey
Whipped cream (See page 194)

To make shortcake, combine flour, baking powder, and salt in a medium bowl. Stir in milk, butter, and 2 tablespoons honey or maple syrup. Batter will be stiff. Distribute evenly into an oiled 8 x 8-inch baking dish. Bake at 425° for about 15 minutes or until inserted toothpick comes out clean.

Meanwhile, combine strawberries and 1/2 cup honey. Mash the strawberries a little to form some juice. (We use a potato masher.)

Cut cake into nine pieces and place shortcake squares in individual bowls. Pour strawberry mixture over the squares and top with whipped cream.

Serves 9

~ This strawberry shortcake recipe always receives a heaping portion of compliments. One of the secrets is the buttery, slightly sweet shortcake. The other secret is fresh, ripe strawberries. When strawberry season rolls around, why not find a farm that has pick-your-own strawberries? Take a picnic lunch and enjoy spending the day in the strawberry fields with family or friends.

YUM YUM BALLS*

1/2 cup natural peanut butter
2 cups unsweetened shredded coconut
1/4 cup chopped walnuts or cashews
1 Tbsp orange juice
1/2 cup chopped dates
1/2 cup raw sunflower seeds
1/4 cup raw honey or brown rice syrup

Combine all ingredients and mix well. Roll into 1-inch balls. Place on ungreased cookie sheet and refrigerate until firm. Store in closed container in refrigerator.

Makes 2-1/2 dozen

~ Why feed your kids candy bars when they can eat these? They satisfy the sweet tooth and provide energy from real food, instead of a sugar-chemical mixture.

* Recipe Contributed by Avis Rowell and Judy Pinard

Fruit Icee

2 cups frozen fruit
1/8 to 1/4 cup honey
4 Tbsp fresh lemon juice
1/2 cup water

Place all ingredients in blender and puree.

Serves two

BEVERAGES

ALMOND MILK*

1 cup raw almonds
   Water
15 small dates or 8 medjool dates
   Small piece of one vanilla bean, optional

Place almonds in a glass bowl with 2 cups water. Allow almonds to soak overnight, or about 8 hours. Drain and rinse thoroughly.

Place almonds and 4 cups water in a blender. Blend until the mixture is completely white and smooth. (No chunks of almonds should remain.)

Place a strainer over a bowl. Place a piece of cheesecloth or a cotton napkin in the strainer. Pour the almond-water mixture through. What is left in the bowl is the almond milk. (The almond pulp can be discarded or kept for use in another recipe. Some people use this pulp as a gluten-free wheat flour substitute.)

Pit dates. Place milk, dates, and piece of vanilla bean in blender; blend well. Voilà! You have fresh almond milk.

~ Almond milk is delicious when poured into a bowl with fresh fruit and cinnamon. You can also freeze the almond milk, and then blend it with frozen fruit to make ice cream. Or, just pour into a glass and enjoy. Yum!

* Recipe Contributed by Keter Shapiro

Sweeten with Fruit

Fruit is a great way to sweeten foods when baking and cooking and preparing beverages. Experiment with pineapple, apple, and orange juices, dates, bananas and applesauce.

APPLE CIDER VINEGAR DRINK

1 Tbsp organic, raw, unfiltered apple cider vinegar
1 Tbsp raw honey
8 oz pure water

Mix together all ingredients and enjoy.

~ Need a pick-me-up in the middle of the afternoon? Forget the soda and go for this drink instead. It is a great energy booster.

Change for the Better

When we were first married, we ate quite differently than we do now. Bill liked Spam sandwiches and thought nothing of eating a pound of bacon at one sitting. Sylvia ate crème horns and candy bars. Typical financially challenged newlyweds, we feasted on fast food, considering taste and cost more than health.

We are living proof that people's taste buds can change because we no longer like many of the unhealthy foods we once ate. We are still not where we want to be; we are not at the end of our journey. But when we reminisce, we realize how far we have come.

If you can't imagine life without your special treats and comfort foods – though you know they are not good for your health – make small but purposeful changes. Dietary changes tend to be permanent rather than temporary when decisions are conscious and deliberate instead of emotional and impulsive.

APRICOT PEACH SMOOTHIE

2 peaches, peeled, seeds removed
4 apricots, peeled, seeds removed
2 bananas
1 cup fresh orange or apple juice
4 ice cubes

In a blender combine peaches, apricots, bananas, and juice. Add ice cubes and pulse.

Serves 2

Who Should Feed the Kids?

Many women view cooking as a necessary bother. The quicker they get it done, the better; they have more important things to do. It's okay if the kids have a bag of potato chips for lunch or eat fast food four or five times a week.

Though many deem homemaking as archaic, it is not a cultural value that should be tossed aside lightly. It is a *biblical* value. Biblical values do not change according to society's shifting trends. Homemaking is not a deviation from the norm; rather, it is a *return* to the biblical norm.

Women have been entrusted with homemaking, of which meal preparation is a vital component. Even if you must work outside the home, you can plan and prepare healthy meals. Rich satisfaction comes from knowing your family is benefiting from your homemaking skills.

BERRY SHAKES

2-1/2 cups frozen berries, slightly thawed
   1 banana, if desired
   1 cup goat yogurt or plain cow's milk yogurt
 1/4 cup organic raw milk or commercial whole milk
2-1/2 Tbsp honey
   4 ice cubes

Measure all ingredients except honey and ice cubes into blender.

With blender running, drizzle honey into shake mixture. Process until smooth. Add ice cubes and pulse until adequately crushed. Pour and enjoy!

Makes 2 1-3/4 cup shakes

~ Let your taste buds help you choose what kind of shake you will make. Strawberries, raspberries, blueberries, mixed berries, and peaches are all delicious and nutritious choices.

~ For convenience, this recipe calls for frozen berries but locally grown, organic, in-season berries are preferred.

~ Depending on how thick you like your shakes, you can adjust the amount of milk and/or yogurt.

~ We really like these shakes. Sometimes we have them for breakfast or as an afternoon snack. Because they are both creamy and icy, on hot summer days they seem to taste even better!

BLUEBERRY ENERGY SHAKE

1 cup milk
1 cup blueberries
1 banana
1 scoop protein powder

Thoroughly blend all ingredients. Serve immediately.

Serves 1

The Homeowner

I live by this simple idea: I do not own my body; God does. I am the caretaker; He is the Homeowner. As caretaker, I am responsible for keeping the house clean and in order.

In spite of my best efforts, however, sometimes things happen over which I have no control. For example, torrential rains may cause the basement to flood. Or a storm may damage the roof. Or perhaps, since I am a fallible human being, I overlook or procrastinate about a needed repair and damage occurs as a result.

When things happen that are out of my control, or when I fail in my responsibilities, I lean on the strength and resources of the Homeowner. He will take action to repair the house. I will do what I can to help with the restoration.

God is kind and understanding, full of compassion. Throughout life, and during our pursuit of better health, it is imperative that we remember that we do what we can do, but when our good is not good enough, He is!

CAROB-COCOA DRINK (HOT)

2 cups milk
1 Tbsp unsweetened cocoa powder
1 Tbsp carob powder
1 Tbsp natural sweetener of choice, or to taste
1 tsp pure vanilla extract, optional
1/2 tsp cinnamon, optional
    Pinch sea salt, optional

Heat milk in a small saucepan until hot. (Do not boil.) Reduce heat to low and whisk in all other ingredients.

Pour and enjoy. The carob-cocoa mixture tends to settle to the bottom of the cup, so serve with a spoon.

Serves 2

~ This is a great transitional drink. In time, you might discover that you prefer to eliminate cocoa powder from this recipe and use only carob powder.

~ Carob powder is not expensive.

~ Carob trees are native to the Mediterranean area and were useful during Bible times. Bill picked carob pods from carob trees in the Middle East. Carob pods are long, flat, dark brown, and earthy tasting.

~ The color and baking properties of carob are similar to cocoa. (Carob chips can be used instead of chocolate chips.) Carob, however, does not have the same flavor as cocoa. Neither does it contain caffeine. It is low in fat and high in protein and important vitamins.

CARROT JUICE

8 carrots, unpeeled and sliced
1 apple, seeded and sliced
1 beet, sliced
1/2 cup green vegetable such as broccoli or spinach
    1/2-inch square piece of ginger, peeled

Place all ingredients in juicer and mix; strain if necessary and drink immediately.

Serves 2

~ If at all possible, use only organic ingredients.

Drink your Vegetables

A good way to get healthy doses of fruits and vegetables is to drink them. Blending or juicing produce amplifies the amount of vitamins you ingest during the day. These are drinkable meals. Depending on your nutritional needs, you can juice anything from apples to blueberries to cucumbers to dandelion greens.

We suggest buying a juicer that retains at least some pulp. The fiber in the pulp helps offset the fructose (which can cause blood sugar spikes).

Some people opt to use a high powered blender. Though pricey, the Vita-Mix is a superb choice.

CLEANSING LEMON DRINK

2 Tbsp pure lemon juice (about 1/2 of a lemon)
(Limes may be used in place of lemons.)
1 to 2 Tbsp pure grade B maple syrup
1/10 tsp cayenne pepper
8 oz distilled or purified water

Stir together all ingredients. Drink 6 to 12 glasses a day. No other foods should be eaten while cleansing with this drink.

This drink cleanses the colon, removing toxins in the body. This regimen may be followed for 1 to 3 days. (Some nutritionists recommend it for a longer cleanse, up to 10 days.) If you have a few days of overindulgence, as often happens during holidays, use this drink to let your body rest and detoxify.

If you use this for a lengthy cleanse, when the cleansing period is over, eat homemade broths and raw fruits and vegetables for several days. Slowly incorporate cooked foods back into your diet. Chew small amounts of healthy food slowly and thoroughly.

What you do after the cleanse often requires greater discipline than the cleanse itself. If you were eating unhealthily prior to the cleanse, alter your food choices to help keep your body clean and toxin-free. Times of cleansing should motivate us to embrace a healthier lifestyle and consume foods that are good for us.

FRUIT SMOOTHIES

6 oz fruit, fresh or frozen
6 oz plain yogurt
1 tsp vanilla
4 Tbsp honey
1/2 cup ice cubes

In a blender, combine fruit, yogurt, vanilla, and honey. Add ice cubes and pulse. Serve immediately.

Serves 2

Eat Real Food

It continually amazes us that people choose manmade foods over natural foods. "The media says ABC natural food is bad. They must be right. I'll eat this chemical substitute instead."

The problem is that media's ideas change like the wind. Some logical people put their brains in neutral when it comes to nutrition. They have such trust in the media that they never stop to examine if what they are being told is the truth.

Think for yourself. When man creates a food in the laboratory or tampers with God's design, that food will have drawbacks. You just can't improve on perfection! The safest route is to choose natural, God-created foods, regardless of the media's power of persuasion.

PINEAPPLE MANGO SHAKES

1-1/2 cups crushed pineapple
   1 mango, peeled and sliccd
  3/4 cup milk
   2 tsp honey
   8 ice cubes

In a blender, combine pineapple, mango, milk, and honey. Add ice cubes and pulse. Serves 2

Piles of Smiles

After starting a new diet, I changed my drive to town to avoid passing my favorite bakery.

I accidentally drove by the bakery this morning, and there in the window was a collection of all my favorite goodies.

I felt this was no accident, so I started to pray.

"God, it's up to you. If you want me to have any of these delicious goodies, create a parking space for me directly in front of the bakery."

Sure enough, He answered my prayer. On my eighth trip around the block, a space opened up.

Karen Ann Bland, Gove, Kansas
"Overheard at the Country Café"
Country Magazine, Aug/Sept 2008, p. 56

WHEY PROTEIN SHAKES

12 oz organic raw milk
  1 scoop whey protein
  1 Tbsp organic cocoa powder
  1 Tbsp natural sweetener of choice

In a blender, mix together all ingredients.

Serves 2

~ If organic raw milk is unavailable, at least purchase milk that is organic. Even if it is pasteurized and homogenized, organic milk is a step above regular milk.

~ Not all whey protein powders are created equal. Look for whey protein that has not been denatured and is from a pure source (i.e. the cows grazed on pesticide and chemical-free grass and were not subjected to hormone treatments). Some whey protein is sweetened with stevia, which is a safe herbal sweetener.

~ Some whey proteins come in flavors such as chocolate, vanilla, strawberry, and raspberry.

~ We sometimes add whey protein to our fruit smoothies for an added nutritional boost.

Lemonade

1 cup fresh squeezed lemon juice, including pulp
3/4 cup raw honey
5 cups pure water

Mix together lemon juice, honey, and water, till honey is dissolved. Pour over ice cubes and serve.

IMPORTANT EXTRAS

BÉCHAMEL SAUCE

3 Tbsp butter
3 Tbsp whole wheat flour, finely ground
2 cups milk
3/4 tsp salt
1/4 tsp white pepper
    A pinch of nutmeg

Bring water in bottom of double boiler to a boil. Melt butter in top of double boiler. Stir in flour with wooden spoon, until smooth. Add milk gradually; stir constantly. Cook until sauce is thick; stir in salt, pepper, and nutmeg.

Remove top of double boiler from water. (If sauce is lumpy, strain through a sieve.) Use as desired.

Pour any remaining sauce into small bowl and refrigerate for future use. For thicker sauce, increase flour to 4 tablespoons.

Makes 2 cups

~ If you do not have a double boiler, follow this same procedure with a heavy bottomed pot over low heat.

~ This traditional sauce with a long history is used by chefs as a basis for other sauces. Louis de Béchameil of 17th century France is credited with perfecting this white cream sauce. The Duke of Escars gave him this backhanded compliment: "That fellow Béchameil has all the luck! I was serving breast of chicken à la crème twenty years before he was born, but I have never had the chance of giving my name to even the most insignificant sauce." For the home cook, béchamel can enhance fish, chicken, eggs, potatoes, lasagna, creamed spinach, and homemade macaroni and cheese.

BILL'S SPICY PEPPER SEASONING

1/8 tsp cayenne pepper
1/4 tsp black pepper
1/4 tsp crushed red pepper flakes
1/2 tsp onion powder
1/2 tsp garlic powder
1/2 tsp mustard powder
  1 tsp sweet paprika
1/4 tsp sea salt, optional

Mix together all ingredients.

Makes 5 teaspoons

~ Use this seasoning to give plain foods pizzazz. Sprinkle it on fish, chicken, beef, and vegetables before baking, broiling, or grilling. Use it instead of salt. Too hot? Cut back on pepper or double other ingredients.

Seasoned with Contentment

People dissatisfied with their possessions are miserable. Instead of complaining because you don't have a new this or that, be thankful for what you do have. To many people in the world, the things you have are only a dream. No one receives lasting happiness from material possessions. Cars get old, clothes go out of style, and exotic vacations become just memories. There is nothing wrong with owning things. What's wrong is when things own us.

"But godliness with contentment is great gain. For we brought nothing into this world, and it is certain we can carry nothing out. And having food and raiment let us be therewith content."
I Timothy 6:6-8

BUTTER

Heavy cream, preferably from organic raw milk
Salt

Step One
Choose your modern butter churn. You can use a food processor or stand mixer. If you have neither of these, you can use a bowl and whisk or a jar. No matter what you use, the general principle is the same: The cream must be agitated until butter forms. (If you use a whisk or jar, anticipate your muscles getting a good workout!)

Step Two
Place cream in the mixing container. (If using a jar, fill it about 1/3 full of cream and tightly cap the jar.)

Step Three
Process or mix the cream; or whisk vigorously; or shake the jar vigorously. Before the cream becomes butter, it will pass through the stage of whipped cream, and then become globules of butterfat.

Step Four
When the globules of butterfat begin to separate, buttermilk will slosh in the bowl or jar. At this point, drain the buttermilk and continue mixing to fully separate. (Use the buttermilk, perhaps in buttermilk pancakes or biscuits.) Drain. Continue mixing and draining until all buttermilk has been extruded.

Step Five
Rinse the butter with cold water. Use a wooden spoon to work all the water out of the butter or lightly knead it with your hands. Remove all water from bowl. This rinsing process will help remove any remaining buttermilk, improving flavor and increasing shelf life.

BUTTER (Cont.)

Step Six
Knead a little salt into the butter to preserve it. Unsalted butter can be kept in the refrigerator for 2 to 3 days, salted butter for 2 to 3 weeks. (Butter can also be frozen.) If desired, you can now gently mix in herbs or honey. Tightly pack butter in glass or ceramic container.

1 cup cream will yield approximately 1/2 cup butter and 1/2 cup buttermilk. If you want more butter, simply use more cream.

~ Some people might wonder why they should make butter when they can buy it at the store. The reason is freshness and taste. The creamy taste of homemade butter is delightful. Plus, it is fun to watch butter form before your eyes!

~ Joan Gussow, author of *This Organic Life*, is quoted as saying, "As for butter versus margarine, I trust cows more than chemists." Indeed, it was a French chemist who, in 1869, invented margarine. Mark Twain also denounced margarine, calling it "another sign of the artificiality of modern life."

Honey Butter

2 Tbsp honey
4 Tbsp softened butter
1/4 tsp cinnamon, or to taste
2 dashes salt, if desired

Combine all ingredients.
Store in refrigerator until ready to serve.

Spread on homemade whole grain bread or rolls.

CAJUN SEASONING

2 Tbsp sweet paprika
2 tsp sea salt
1 tsp cayenne pepper
2 tsp onion powder
2 tsp garlic powder
3/4 tsp black pepper
3/4 tsp white pepper
3/4 tsp thyme leaves, crushed
3/4 tsp sweet basil leaves, crushed
3/4 tsp oregano leaves, crushed
1 tsp mustard powder
1-1/2 tsp unrefined sugar

Combine all ingredients and store in a tightly sealed container.

Makes 1/4 cup

~ This seasoning blend is hot and spicy. Use it on fish, burgers, eggs, vegetables...the sky is the limit.

~ "Mustard powder" is the same as "dry mustard" and "ground mustard."

Honey Mustard

1/4 cup yellow mustard
1/4 cup raw honey
1/2 cup mayonnaise

In a small bowl, combine all ingredients. Chill for one hour before serving. Use as a dipping sauce for chicken tenders or as a salad dressing.

Makes one cup

CARAMELIZED ONIONS

1 Tbsp olive oil
3 onions, cut into thinly sliced rings
2 tsp balsamic vinegar

In heavy skillet, heat oil on low to medium heat. Add onions and stir to coat onions with oil. Simmer slowly till onions are browned, about 30 to 45 minutes. If after the first 20 to 30 minutes, you find onions are on verge of burning, add a little more oil. Stir often and scrape bottom of pan with metal spatula to prevent burning.

Onions should be a rich brown color before stirring in balsamic vinegar. Once onions have browned, stir in vinegar to coat onions and scrape bottom of pan to deglaze. Continue to simmer, uncovered, for 5 to 10 more minutes. Do not allow onions to burn.

~ Caramelized onions are especially good on hamburgers or turkey burgers. You can also put them on homemade pizzas, add them to roasted or mashed potatoes, or make them the star ingredient of a quiche. Put them in omelets or add them to casseroles. Some people like to pair them with a mild, soft cheese. Put them on sandwiches, use them in French onion soup, top salmon with them, and toss them with pasta. The delicious possibilities are endless!

Caramelization

Caramelizing is a cooking process that brings out natural sweetness in foods. Foods are cooked over low to medium-low heat and allowed to brown. Caramelized foods enhance otherwise ordinary dishes. Some people add sucanat or turbinado sugar to the onions to speed the process.

CREAM CHEESE FROSTING

2 8-oz packages organic cream cheese, softened
1 cup butter, softened
1 tsp vanilla
2 Tbsp lemon juice
1/2 cup honey

Whip cream cheese and butter with electric mixer. Add vanilla, lemon juice, and honey. Whip 1 to 2 minutes until smooth.

For smaller needs:
4 oz cream cheese, softened
1/4 cup butter, softened
1/4 tsp vanilla
1/2 Tbsp lemon juice
2 Tbsp honey

$ Money Saving Tip $

Invest in quality kitchen equipment.

As you can afford them, stock your kitchen with the following: blender, mixer, juicer, grain mill, quality pots and pans, high-grade measuring utensils, sprouting tray or jars, and dehydrator.

A home cook investing in good kitchen equipment is like a landscaper investing in mowing and trimming equipment. To get the job done properly, you simply need the right tools. Your investment will yield great future dividends!

DILLY BEANS

3 lb green beans
6 pint jars
6 garlic cloves
6 Tbsp fresh dill
1-1/2 tsp cayenne pepper or crushed red pepper
1-3/4 cup white vinegar
1-3/4 cup apple cider vinegar
3-1/2 cups water
6 Tbsp salt

Wash beans thoroughly. Drain water and snap off ends of beans. Pack lengthwise into clean, hot jars. To each jar add 1 clove garlic, 1 tablespoon fresh dill, and 1/4 teaspoon cayenne pepper or crushed red pepper.

In saucepan, mix vinegars, water, and salt; bring to a boil. Pour the hot vinegar mixture over beans, leaving 1/2-inch headspace. Seal jars and place them in boiling water for 5 minutes. Remove jars, tighten lids, and set jars several inches apart to cool.

~ These beans are delicious. They arc crispy and the vinegars give them a delightful mouthwatering zing.

Presidential Pickles

"On a hot day in Virginia, I know nothing more comforting than a fine spiced pickle, brought up trout-like from the sparkling depths of the aromatic jar below the stairs of Aunt Sally's cellar."

Thomas Jefferson

HOMEMADE YOGURT

1 quart organic raw milk
2 Tbsp yogurt for starter (good commercial yogurt)
1 quart Mason canning jar
1 meat thermometer

Note: You cannot buy raw milk in some states. This recipe is for making yogurt with organic raw (unpasteurized and unhomogenized) milk. When working with raw milk keep things very clean. Raw milk is not the big bad monster the government makes it out to be. We have been drinking raw milk for about 8 years and have never had one problem with it. In fact, raw milk from a good source is much healthier than store bought (pasteurized, homogenized) milk. However, we believe it pays to be safe. Be sure to boil canning jars, lids and utensils that you are using. We keep a pot of 180° to 200° water on the stove while making yogurt to dip utensils and thermometer in after each use.

Step One
Pour one quart raw milk in top of double boiler. Put about an inch of water in the bottom of double boiler. Bring milk slowly to 110°. Do not allow heat to exceed 110° or heat will begin to destroy enzymes in the yogurt.

Step Two
Add one tablespoon commercial yogurt (we use Redwood Hill Farm plain goat yogurt) to the milk and stir till dissolved.

Step Three
Make sure quart-sized jar has cooled from being boiled. Pour milk into jar and add one more tablespoon of yogurt; stir till almost dissolved. Place lid on tightly.

HOMEMADE YOGURT (Cont.)

Step Four
Fill clean plastic cooler (ice chest) with 100° water, 1/2 inch below the bottom of the ring of the jar, approximately 6 inches high. Place jar in cooler, making sure the water is not over the bottom of the ring. Close chest and let set for 12 hours. During the 12 hours and until yogurt has cooled, do not jostle or shake the yogurt. This will disturb the proliferation process.

Step Five
After 12 hours, move yogurt to refrigerator and let set for a day. The longer the yogurt sets the more tart it will become. When opening jar, use whisk to stir in cream that has risen to the top.

Makes 1 quart

Serving Suggestions: Sweeten yogurt with pure maple syrup and enjoy. We think this must surely be one of the most delicious foods on the planet! You can also mix berries and Granola (See page 61) into the yogurt. Use it for making Berry Shakes (page 169), Fruit Smoothies (page 174), and Swiss Müesli (page 62).

~ If yogurt is not thick enough to suit you, do not use more starter the next time; use less. Skip Step 2 and stir only one tablespoon of starter into milk after it has been poured into the jar. The bacteria need room to grow so less starter will make thicker yogurt.

~ Once you have made your first batch of yogurt you can reserve a little yogurt from that batch to use as starter for your next quart.

LABENAH

8 cups plain organic yogurt
1/2 tsp sea salt
2 Tbsp olive oil

Select a large bowl and a colander that can rest on the rim of the bowl. Thoroughly clean colander and bowl then pour boiling water over them to sterilize. Allow to air dry thoroughly.

Line the colander with several layers of cheesecloth. Secure the cheesecloth so that its edges will not fall into the colander.

In a separate bowl, stir salt into the yogurt. Pour the salted yogurt into the cheesecloth.

Leave the yogurt at room temperature for 12 to 24 hours, allowing all liquid to drain into the bowl. The longer it drains, the thicker it will become. (The liquid is whey and what is left in the strainer is the cheese.)

Gently remove the cheese from the cheesecloth and transfer to a bowl. Stir in the olive oil. Store in a covered container in the refrigerator.

Makes about 2 cups

~ This is the Middle Eastern version of cream cheese. It is delicious and so easy to make! Try it plain on lightly toasted pita bread (yum!) or spread it on a whole grain baguette with tomatoes, cucumbers, olives, and mint.

~ We were introduced to labenah while in the country of Jordan. Turkish labenah was our favorite type of labenah. This recipe tastes quite similar to it.

LACTIC ACID FERMENTED CUCUMBERS
(Old Fashioned Dill Pickles)

4 to 6 pickling cucumbers
   3 Tbsp fresh dill
 1/2 tsp mustard seed
   6 cloves fresh garlic
   1 Tbsp sea salt (We recommend Celtic sea salt.)
   4 Tbsp whey (If unavailable, add 1 more Tbsp salt.)
   1 cup filtered water
      (Do not use tap water; the chlorine will destroy
      the fermentation process. If filtered water is
      unavailable, boil tap water and let it cool to
      room temperature before using.)

Step One
Place fresh dill, mustard seed and garlic into quart size canning jar.

Step Two
Wash cucumbers in cool water to remove excess dirt. Cut them in half lengthwise and pack them firmly into jar so the pickles can't rise above the pickling solution.

Step Three
Pour water into jar, leaving about 1-1/2 inches at the top. Add whey and/or sea salt. If cucumbers are not completely covered, add a little more water. Leave at least 1 inch of space at the top of the jar.

Step Four
Place canning lid on tightly and shake a little to start dissolving the salt.

Step Five
Leave at room temperature for three days. Then place in refrigerator to slow fermentation process. After three weeks, open and enjoy. If pickles are not sour enough yet, allow them another week or so in the refrigerator.

LACTIC ACID FERMENTED CUCUMBERS (Cont.)

Makes 1 quart

~ Note: If cucumbers have lost their firmness before pickling, place them in cold filtered water for a few hours and they will become firm again.

~ This is Bill's tried and true recipe. Crispy, crunchy, and just the right amount of sour...yum!

Lactic Acid Fermentation

In many societies, and for many generations, lactic acid fermentation has been a common and safe method of food preservation. Lactic acid fermentation utilizes the lactic acid bacteria naturally present in plants and milk products, whereas "fermentation" requires the addition of bacterial culture to initiate the fermentation process.

Lactic acid fermentation increases nutrient absorption and proliferates healthy bacteria, while inhibiting unfriendly bacteria. This process benefits digestion, boosts metabolism, supports systems that are lactose intolerant, and fights cancer.

Cabbage fermented by this process is used to make sauerkraut and kimchi in the same way cucumbers are made into lactic acid fermented pickles. Milk products can be fermented into healthy cheeses, yogurt, and kefir. Grains, beans, and even fish can be fermented.

MAYONNAISE

2 eggs
1/2 tsp sea salt
1/8 to 1/2 tsp cayenne pepper, optional
1/4 tsp paprika, optional
1 Tbsp honey
3 Tbsp vinegar or lemon juice
(or 1-1/2 Tbsp each)
2 cups safflower or sunflower oil

Note: Place the oil in the refrigerator at least several hours before making the mayonnaise. *Cold* oil makes better mayonnaise. Also, use expeller pressed oil.

In a blender, beat the eggs. Add all other ingredients, except the oil, and blend for a few more seconds.

With blender on, add the oil *very* slowly. The mixture will become thicker as more oil is added, but it *must* be only a thin stream. Blend mixture until thick. (Pouring the oil in slowly will take at least five minutes.)

Pour mayonnaise into a glass container and refrigerate to thicken further. It can be kept in refrigerator for up to two weeks.

Makes 2 cups

~ If I know that I will be using my mayonnaise for something like chocolate cake, I omit the cayenne pepper and paprika to avoid a clash of flavors.

~ Some people worry about using raw egg in mayonnaise. Stop to consider that your cookie and cake batters have raw egg in them. You probably allow your children or grandchildren to lick the spoon or bowl and never think about raw egg remnants they ingest. Using lemon or vinegar in the mayonnaise will help combat any negative effects of raw eggs. If it is any consolation, this mayonnaise has never made us sick.

PIZZA SAUCE

1 Tbsp olive oil
2 tsp minced garlic
1 medium onion, finely chopped
2 32-oz cans crushed fire roasted tomatoes, undrained
1 6-oz can tomato paste
3 Tbsp honey
3 Tbsp water
1/2 tsp sea salt
1/2 tsp crushed red pepper
1 tsp black pepper
1 tsp dried oregano
1 Tbsp dried sweet basil
3 bay leaves

Using medium pot, heat olive oil on low to medium heat. Add garlic, then onions; cook till translucent. Add all other ingredients. Bring to boil, then reduce heat to low and cook, covered, for 1 to 2 hours. Stir occasionally.

Makes approximately 8 cups

~ For best flavor, prepare sauce the day before using it.

~ This sauce can be frozen for later use. It can also be used to make calzones or as a spaghetti sauce.

~ See page 130 for pizza-making suggestions.

Value the Gift of Good Food

"If the divine creator has taken pains to give us
delicious and exquisite things to eat,
the least we can do is prepare them well
and serve them with ceremony."

Fernand Point

THAI PEANUT SAUCE

1/2 cup organic coconut milk (not coconut cream)
3/4 cup freshly ground peanut butter
1 Tbsp organic Worcestershire sauce
1-1/2 Tbsp molasses
2 Tbsp honey
2 Tbsp freshly squeezed lime juice
2 Tbsp shoyu soy sauce
2 Tbsp fish sauce
3 Tbsp sweet chilli sauce
1/8 tsp (or to taste) hot and spicy chilli oil
1/8 tsp crushed red pepper
1/4 tsp cumin
1/4 tsp turmeric

In a small bowl, stir together all ingredients and chill.

Makes 2 cups

~ This is especially good served with Chicken Lettuce Wraps (See page 118) and Chicken Satay (See page 119). It can also be used as a dip for carrot sticks.

Tomato Equivalents

2 cups tomato sauce =
3/4 cup tomato paste + 1-1/4 cups water

1 cup firmly packed tomatoes =
1/2 cup tomato sauce + 1/2 cup water

1 cup canned tomatoes =
1-1/2 cups fresh, chopped tomatoes,
simmered 10 minutes

1/2 cup tomato paste =
1 cup tomato sauce, simmered till reduced by half

WHIPPED CREAM

1 cup cream
  Pinch of salt
2 Tbsp honey
1/2 tsp vanilla

Chill stainless steel bowl and electric mixer beaters about 15 minutes. Pour cream in bowl and add salt; beat on medium speed until soft peaks form. Add honey and vanilla; beat to combine. Keep chilled.

Makes 2 cups

~ Homemade whipped cream is easy to make and dreamily delicious. It's the real deal! You'll probably never again buy that stuff in the tub; this tastes so much better.

~ Make sure you don't beat the cream too long or you will have butter instead of whipped cream.

Measurement Equivalents

3 teaspoons = 1 tablespoon

1/4 cup = 4 tablespoons
1/3 cup = 5-1/2 tablespoons
1/2 cup = 8 tablespoons
3/4 cup = 12 tablespoons
1 cup = 16 tablespoons

1 cup = 1/2 pint = 8 oz
2 cups = 1 pint = 16 oz
4 cups = 2 pints = 1 quart
16 cups = 8 pints = 4 quarts = 1 gallon

1 pound = 16 ounces

INDEX